Jesus Beyond Religion
The Truth that Sets You Free

Bruce W. MacCullough

Jesus Beyond Religion: The Truth that Sets You Free

Book designed by David Kudler and Stillpoint Digital Press
(stillpointdigital.com)

Dedicated to

my wife and children

Noreen, Allison, Andrea, & Amanda

They help make life beautiful and full

Contents

Preface

As I finish this book, we are deep into two new history-making events. There is the coronavirus pandemic, COVID-19, as well as the harsh police killing of George Floyd, which ignited large scale protests and unrest across the United States for weeks now, also launching protests in other countries. The pandemic quickly became global, rendering us one world in common struggle. Nations are striving and sharing together. People have been thrown back to a simpler existence, compelled to quarantine, with many struggling or suffering. In the midst of this crisis, we witness a large and broad wave of compassion as so many people respond to the needs of those sick or hurting, with heightened gratitude for those serving on the front lines. Crises bring out the best in so many.

Just as we were making progress with the pandemic, the video of the slow, inhumane choking death of George Floyd went viral. It rocked the world. People everywhere, particularly young people, exploded. The underlying pain of decades— nay, centuries—of racial inequality and oppression, erupted like an earthquake. Aftershocks have continued for weeks. Sadly, it required a painful tragedy to magnify the festering wounds of injustice, to provide the impetus and fuel needed to rise up and create change. This moment is still rumbling, with the changes just starting to unfold.

This book emerged in the spring of 2019 before these two world moments. It arose out of my lifelong journey of faith, driven by an exhilarating and passionate sense of the relevant and liberating message and ministry of Jesus containing "the truth that sets you free." Jesus continues to bring us a message relevant to this time, a message of love and forgiveness as the source and power for a Way of life that calls us to help others, especially those whom he called "the least of these my brothers (and sisters)," as well as to live out the prophetic call to "do justice and love mercy."

Yes, we are one world under one God. In Jesus it is revealed that God suffers with us, rather than remaining the remote, unchangeable, unfeeling deity of abstract philosophies. Suffering and love are the deepest experiences of life, touching everyone of us. God feels our pain, and He calls and journeys with us to overcome suffering and adversity. "God is love" declare the scriptures, forgiving and inviting us to love one another, with all that that entails.

In this book I take a close look at the person of Jesus as revealed in scripture, and endeavor to extract and lift up the heart of his message and work. Others have done this before, but I am convinced that we have to do so repeatedly, because the dross and weeds of formalized religion, fanatical religion, and theological and doctrinal excess continually return, strangling the life, joy, and vitality of the wonderful message of Jesus. Even as Jesus declared in his time that there needed to be "new wineskins" for the new wine of his season, so also in ours, in this ripe moment.

Introduction

Throughout the United States and Europe there are numerous traditional Christian churches that are like little 'Titanics'. They are sinking slowly while the remaining members say "strike up the band," resigned to going under. Organized religion faces challenges from within and without. Not enough are asking: Is there any hope? Is there anything that can be done? For the original Titanic help was too far away. I assert that there is hope and help. This book is a clarion call to step up, look outward, and find new rescue ships of hope on the horizon!

We are accelerating into the future. The pace of change is increasing—astonishing technologies; perpetual upgrades; medical discoveries with both exciting and controversial capabilities; political chaos; new, unusual, and dangerous leaders; new and evolving problems; the world shrinking around us. If we don't stick our heads in the ground, reality can come at us like a pack of wolves. Old ideas, old worldviews, old solutions cease to provide adequate answers and solutions. All of this shakes the foundations. What can be done? How can or does one find a code, a philosophy, a faith to live by?

In the writing of this book, Jesus' teaching about old and new or fresh wineskins has risen up with power, and captured my imagination. It was a key part of his religion-altering message in his day, and I believe it is once again a transformative message for change now.

Jesus may well be the most written-about person in human history. It should cause every author to ask, "Why should you write another book on Jesus? Will it be beneficial and insightful rather than simply adding to the confusing multitude of books, sects, and preachers?" I join with those who are already on this path of rethinking how we do church and discipleship in the 21st century, and who are declaring that this is a time for renewal, or awakening—a time for new wineskins! I strive, yearn, and pray that this book will contribute to this new envisioning, one that will reach out to the many people who have left religion to participate in the inspiring discussion of Jesus beyond religion.

A survey of the history of Christianity shows that the message and meaning of Jesus frequently gets choked and twisted by the weeds of excessive religious doctrine, ritual and cultural distortion. The one who came to give us the "truth that shall set you free" often gets set on a shelf to be admired, but not followed. Thus there is the need for constant vigilance. That is at least one of the key reasons God has to continually do new things throughout history to get us back on track, from calling the nomad Abraham to go forth and create a new people that will be a light to the nations, to the raising up of prophets that changed the essence of true religion, to the sending of Jesus, the Messiah, as the defining revelation of His purposes. This is a call to study and action towards pursuing God's call in this time. And in this process we can find again the "fullness of life"—human flourishing as some so aptly refer to it—that Jesus demonstrated and taught when he walked this earth.

My intention is to ground this book on a close look at what Jesus said and demonstrated in his actions. It is not a new revelation, yet new in the way that Jesus renewed his Jewish tradition. Though he boldly challenged, even overturned religious practices and beliefs prevalent in his day, he claimed he was being faithful to the true intent of the Law and the Prophets. By Jesus' time, Judaism had already accumulated a large body of law, traditions, and rituals that, he proclaimed, often suffocated the real purpose of the faith. This proclamation is summed up in his statement, "The Sabbath was made for humanity, not humanity for the Sabbath," for there were over 600 Sabbath laws at that time.

To demonstrate that the foundation of this book is taken from Jesus as we know him through the Bible, I include a larger number of biblical quotes in the beginning.

As Jesus often clashed with and rocked the religious establishment of his day, his message changed the emphasis from religious forms and practices to a way of living grounded in the two Great Commandments: to love God and to love your neighbor as yourself. Thus, soon after Jesus' earthly life, his early followers were often called people of "the Way."

As Jesus walked about teaching and healing, it is striking how frequently he was challenged by religious leaders and to whom he responded harshly. His responses often shocked, upset, or enraged them. He proclaimed that actions of love and reconciliation and justice are the first priority, taking precedence over religious ritual and practices. After the religious transformation Jesus laid out, I explore what following Jesus—discipleship—means in our times. I weave in a few stories from my own journey of faith, to keep it down-to-earth and personal, resonating with Jesus' message as foremost a life of Love and a Way of Living.

I believe my assessment of Jesus and his work is closer to what he revealed and called us to than much of current practices and preaching in the world in the plethora of Christian sects. Additionally, I assert that following Jesus should not require a systematic theology, or dense academic explanations. It can and should be compelling and understandable by everyone—the salt of the earth. Jesus chose stories or parables to teach God's Way of life as he walked among the people, constantly invoking teachable moments, healing moments, and saving moments. These stories and actions penetrated into both heart and mind (then and to this day), moving and drawing people into a renewed life and relationship with God. We examine the life and person of Jesus, for it transforms our understanding of God, which is pivotal to the life of faith.

When the Roman Empire adopted Christianity as the religion of the empire in the 4th century, big changes occurred—some of which are indeed troubling—as Christianity began to take on some of the forms of empire. Accompanying this, great Councils were called for the purpose of defining what Christianity is. Through that process, however, Christianity started to become more of a people of the Creeds, focused on a developing and complex theological-philosophical system of doctrine and law. This academic edifice began to take priority, replacing the Way of living by love as Jesus taught. Incredibly, the life and teachings of Jesus did not appear anywhere in the first two Creeds, which are frequently deemed the most important. The result was that the Jesus of history faded into the background and a more conceptual Christ of faith became dominant. To the extent that we lose the Jesus who walked the earth, we abandon the heart and flesh of what he expressly taught and demonstrated! The reputation as people of the Way diminished, and Christianity was centered in creedal orthodoxy. Consequently, in the many centuries since then, and still today, this religion-altering, life-giving and life-changing Way of Jesus has been sidelined, choked, or diverted by religious success and ceremony, in a tsunami of theological and philosophical complexity that smothers the simple core of Christianity.

I therefore start with a "no holds barred" demonstration and discussion of Jesus' clash with many of the religious leaders of his day, then move to how he re-ordered the life of faith, beginning with the forgiveness, reconciliation, and healing, that sets people free from what holds them back, and liberates them to live a life of love. It is indeed Good News that is paradoxical—both simple and easy, yet also profound and hard. Offering us the "Way and the Truth and the Life," he invites us into the "truth that sets you free."

We then move forward to consider what new wineskins might look like, by both looking at newly arisen ministries and initiatives, and imagining other new wineskins. At the end I raise perhaps the pivotal question of Christianity, followed by my Joyful Epilogue.

There will also be a few discussions, which might appear tangential, but I argue that they are pertinent to my overall purpose, and hopefully enlightening and interesting as well.

My main source comes from the scriptures, though adding a number of authors and scholars along the way, but ultimately this is not a piece of academic research—even though I have done considerable study over my lifetime journey of striving to live a faithful life. In this historical moment of exceptional upheaval, crises, and confusion in the world of religion and Christianity, it is appropriate and urgent now to engage Jesus as he presents himself, for it can change how we live and how we understand God and the world.

At this time, as the largest sect in the world, the Roman Catholic church is still struggling with the revelation of an alarming scale of sexual abuse—particularly of tens of thousands of children, along with the criminal cover-up of these crimes. It has happened all over the world, and likely for much longer than we want to know. Recently, widespread sexual misconduct and abuse has come to light in the Southern Baptist church as well, and to some extent across all religion and society.

Quite a few narrow-minded fundamentalist sects are growing, some of which ignore modern science, some presenting a narrow and frightening view of God—a view that does not fit with what Jesus reveals. And tragically, extremist sects are wreaking terror in many places.

In this situation, a fresh reading and discussion of the incredible person and message of Jesus can move us back to the heart of Jesus' message, and what he died and lived for. The word gospel means "Good News." I strive to move away the debris and reveal the very Good news of Jesus that can set us free.

Other authors are now talking about the need for religious change, or religious renewal, of new ways to embrace Christianity or spirituality or faithful living. Diana Butler-Bass' *Christianity After Religion* is a fine book, joining with other voices declaring that we are deep into a "New Spiritual Awakening," the fourth Awakening in American history. I concur, but this book has a different emphasis. Though connecting with the reality of renewal or awakenings in religion, mine is not a sociological-religious discussion, but rather a treatise focused on Jesus and the core meaning of his message and work. Dietrich Bonhoeffer, writer and martyr of the faith in Nazi Germany, was already perceiving and asking similar questions almost a hundred years ago, writing, "What is bothering me incessantly is the question what Christianity really is, or indeed who Christ really is, for us today. . . . We are moving toward a completely religionless time; people as they are now simply cannot be religious anymore[1]. . .What does that mean for Christianity? If religion is only a garment of Christianity—and even this garment has looked very different at different times—then what is a religionless Christianity?"[2]

Though Bonhoeffer was speaking out of a troubled European context in the previous century, presently throughout the West people continue to turn away from religion. It is worth pondering that in some parts of the world, like Africa and parts of Latin America, religion is still strong and even growing. Yet in the West, both the United States and Europe, Bonhoeffer's questions are still relevant. I argue that Jesus endures through the clouds of confusion, the blinding smoke of conflict, and the fog of hopelessness, and re-emerges above the weeds of religion with a message and vision of love, resurrection, and new life.

To the reader without much interest in a religious book or

---

1   Pugh, Jeffrey C., and Martin E. Marty. 2009. *Religionless Christianity: Dietrich Bonhoeffer in Troubled Times.*, p. 85-6

2   *Ibid.* p. 87

who may have rejected God and religion: You will find that I (and Jesus) am partially with you in rejecting much of religion. What remains is wonderful. We must not throw out the baby with the bath water.

At the end, I offer a discussion of how my significant studies in mathematics and science has not diminished, but rather has supported my faith.

I ask you to consider the gold that I find in the soil of Christianity, beneath all the weeds. I invite you along with me.

At the end of most chapters I have put in some Reflection questions, inviting you to chew and digest what was presented.

Chapter 1. The Problem

And no one puts new wine into old wineskins; otherwise, the wine will burst the skins and the wine is lost, and so are the skins; but one puts new wine into fresh wineskins.
(Mark 2:22)[3]

How many people do you know who say "I don't go to church anymore," or "I rarely attend synagogue. Sometimes I pop in for holidays." Or maybe they refer to the massive sex scandals, or religious terrorists, or religious conflicts and divisions around the world—concluding that religion is more of a problem than a solution. This challenge is not easily dismissed.

Data and polls show that in the western world, religious membership continues to decline for many denominations. There are both religious and nonreligious folk who would like to move religion into a mostly private realm, out of government and the public square, pushing religion onto smaller and smaller "playing fields." This viewpoint is muddied or complicated by the important American tenet of separation of church and state. The founders of our country did not want divine right monarchy or any form of theocracy where religious leaders orchestrate government.

Nevertheless, religious voices have refused to be silenced throughout our history and they remain a force in American society and in politics. Among the most notable is the Rev. Martin Luther King, Jr. Emerging from the harsh realities of slavery, Jim Crow and the subsequent creation of segregated ghettoes of poverty, followers of Dr. King and other civil rights leaders took their faith into the streets and called for justice, drawing on the powerful prophetic messages contained in the Bible "Let justice roll down like waters, and righteousness like a mighty stream" (Amos 5). Following after Dr.

Biblical quotes come from either the Revised Standard Version or the New Revised Standard Version

King, people on both or all sides have been advocating, protesting, and clashing in the public and political sphere, claiming the moral high ground, and declaring God's affirmation. Certainly there are nonreligious folk involved, appealing to what they believe is right, moral and just. All this religious activity and fervor in our western context is now taking place in a world that seems to be moving beyond religion. The future seems unclear. I take a deep look at Jesus as he is revealed in the gospels, and propose that Jesus is calling us out again into new wine for our times, and raising the challenge that the old wineskins cannot contain this new wine.

Many traditional churches look like this: The membership is aging, not many young folk in the pews. Familiar hymns are sung. It is a friendly place. The bulletin announces a nice array of activities, a church supper; a special holiday service soon, volunteer opportunities, and good causes to support financially. Sometimes there is a Minute for Mission, highlighting one of the good missions that the church supports. Pastor Smith gives instructive sermons, teaching about the history and context of a scriptural passage, as well as calling people to step out and help those in need. The church is a caring community, both within and beyond. Of course, all churches and organizations are subject to human foibles and failings, yet overarching that they remain places of compassion and kindness. One could say that the above is a reasonably good "report card," but it is often poor in vitality, life-changing power, and deep engagement with the world—God's world.

Membership and budget have been going down for years. The world beyond the walls—sometimes near, but often far—seems chaotic and deeply troubled. There are too many poor, of which a disproportionate number are people of color. Too many people earn poverty wages, live in dilapidated housing, attend underfunded schools, and live in troubled neighborhoods. Ghettoes and the cycle of poverty continue, leading to dangerous neighborhoods, generational trauma, crime, and incarceration. Poor children from highly stressed family situations and dangerous neighborhoods come to school without a good breakfast—and we wonder why they cannot learn effectively. Some people of faith, and some of no faith, roughly say "I sympathize, I wish it were different, but it is complicated," and they go their way. Those are three seductive words: it is complicated. But if it were our children and grandchildren suffering and deprived, would we still throw up our hands, saying "It is complicated" and walk away?

Every one of these numerous churches does give money and resources and gets involved to help those in need. The sum total of all that giving is large. I would not want to imagine what would happen if all that generosity, along with a massive number of volunteers, were not present and active. Certainly the world would be in far worse shape. Yet the world's large-scale problems persist and the hostilities, conflicts, and divisions are way too many. The pivotal work of reconciliation and justice is sorely needed, both near and far. Indeed, reconciliation is at the heart of Jesus' work and message—and it is a two-sided task— reconciliation between God and people, and also between peoples. More than ever now, it has become evident that reconciliation without justice is deficient. The message of Jesus transforms life and sends us into the world to change hearts and to "love our neighbor as ourselves." Those words are deep and wide, challenging and joyful.

The old church models are not working well. Once again, the old wineskins cannot hold the new wine of the present. Religion is under assault, often deservedly so. The good news of this book is that out of the weeds of religion we find that there is a Jesus beyond religion.

On the one hand, for many denominations the bleeding— the decline—is significant. Therefore, the call and message of this book is urgent. On the other hand, in what follows I raise up the hopeful, challenging, and joyful message and work of Jesus—freed from a mass of religious toxins.

Let's take a close look at Jesus—to be surprised and inspired.

However, before entering more fully into the wonderful news and implications of Jesus, it is necessary in chapter 2 to lay out the harsh challenge that both the prophets and Jesus blasted the religious establishment with.

Reflection Questions

1. Is your faith community facing a decline in membership, resources, or both? Begin a discussion on where you think your faith community is heading.

2. Does your faith community move beyond charity to the challenging work of reconciliation and justice? You can begin this discussion here, or wait till later in this book.

Chapter 2. The Truth that Sets You Free

*Christ has abolished the law with its commandments and or-
dinances, that he might create in himself one new humanity in
place of the two, thus making peace, and might reconcile both
groups (Jews and Gentiles) to God in one body through the cross,
thus putting to death that hostility through it.*
(Ephesians 2:15-16)

Jesus came with a life-changing message. He brought a bold
call for reconciliation between people and God, as well as reconciliation among peoples of the world. Unfortunately, he quickly ran into
opposition. Though the crowds of everyday people who came to hear
him were excited and astonished, many members of the religious
establishment almost immediately began to question, challenge, and
oppose him. Jesus was a Jew, who boldly claimed to be teaching
and living the true essence of the Jewish tradition as new wine for
his time, especially as he built on the religion-changing message of
the Hebrew prophets. To best present both the biblical foundations
of Jesus' teaching, as well as his new wine, it is necessary to bring in
quite a few quotes from scripture at the outset.

Jesus' conflict with the religious establishment was rough,
as well as revealing. Fasten your safety belts as we listen to Jesus un-
leash a litany of "woe unto you" declarations, including these: "Woe
to you scribes and Pharisees, hypocrites! For you lock people out of
the kingdom of heaven. For you do not go in yourselves, and when
others are going in, you stop them" (Matthew 23:13). And, "Woe to
you scribes and Pharisees, hypocrites! For you tithe mint and dill and
cummin, and have neglected the weightier matters of the law, justice
and mercy and faith" (Matthew 23;23).

It is quite clear that the second quote above reflects the
powerful passage from the prophet Micah that culminates with:

> "He has told you, o mortal, what is good:
> and what does the Lord require of you
> but to do justice, and to love kindness (or mercy),
> and to walk humbly with your God"
> (Micah 6:8)

The harshness of some of Jesus' sayings mirror that of the prophets. The examples are numerous, but here is another well known one from Amos. According to Amos the Lord declares:

> "I hate, I despise your festivals,
> and I take no delight in your solemn assemblies . . .
> Even though you offer me your burnt offerings,
> I will not accept them;
> And the offerings of well-being of your fatted animals
> I will not look upon.
> Take away from me the noise of your songs;
> I will not listen to the melody of your harps.
> But let justice roll down like waters,
> And righteousness like an ever-flowing stream."
> (Amos 5:21-24)

We must remind ourselves that 2700 years ago the nations and tribes of peoples believed in a vast array of gods. Each nation had different gods, gods in charge of different aspects of life, and who were quite "human" in how they functioned—generous, angry, jealous, competitive, volatile, erratic, and the like. They floated in the heavens and sometimes would come down and even mate with human beings. Frequently, these gods demanded many things—gold, silver, sacrifices, allegiance, vengeance, etc. The Hebrew prophets proclaimed one supreme God (perhaps not quite ready to say no other gods exist, but moving that way). Remarkably, they received the insight that the essence of the true God's desires and requirements were not like those of the demands of brutal earthly kings and all the false deities modeled after human kings. No, this God harshly rejected all that malignant religiosity and called for kindness, mercy, compassion, and justice, not merely a modification, but truly a revolution in the essence of religion. Jesus clearly referenced and affirmed the message of these prophets—and went beyond.

In the time of Jesus there were hundreds of Sabbath laws, and countless other religious practices and requirements. He relegates these things below the call to live kindly, humbly and justly.

Here is another gem from the prophet Isaiah:

"Is not this the fast that I choose:

to loose the bonds of injustice,

to undo the thongs of the yoke,

to let the oppressed go free,

and to break every yoke?

Is it not to share your bread with the hungry,

And bring the homeless poor into your house;

When you see the naked, to cover them,

And not to hide yourself from your own kin?"

(Isaiah 58: 6-7)

So much of what Jesus taught, was through striking stories (parables) and short ethical teachings. According to the gospel of Luke, Jesus' connection to the Hebrew prophets is so strong that he launched his ministry in a temple with a reading from the prophet Isaiah! "Jesus stood up to read, and the scroll of the prophet Isaiah was given to him. He unrolled the scroll and found the place where it was written:

"The Spirit of the Lord is upon me,

Because he has anointed me

To bring good news to the poor.

He has sent me to proclaim release to the captives

And recovery of sight to the blind,

To let the oppressed go free."

(Luke 4: 16-18)

Thus we see that the Hebrew prophets frequently assailed both the religious establishment of their time and religious ritual and sacrifice, centuries before Jesus. Their challenge and assault on religious ceremony, sacrifice, legalism and misguided leadership is a striking, even startling component of Jesus message as well.

The reader needs to know that there are many more quotes in the prophets on the same themes that I could add, but I believe I have offered enough to make the case quite strong without wearing down the reader. Knowing that there are numerous biblical references on this topic addresses the grave danger of those who pick one or two passages—and with minimal context—to build their theology. A fairly recent case of this was with a popular TV preacher who proclaimed "possibility thinking!" in one form or another, week after week. It is great to be upbeat, but to reduce Christianity to a philosophy of thinking your way to success is wrong.

A friend posed this question: why is it so important to connect Jesus to the prophets? I have three succinct answers. First, Jesus made the connection. Second, we need to remember that Jesus was Jewish, and even though he was seeding big challenges and transformations, he asserted that he was actually teaching and living the essence and true meaning of the Law and the Prophets! Third, the prophets are also deeply connected to the new wine for today, as God's call to us in this time.

Let's look at the broad sweep of Jesus' ministry. Jesus walked through the countryside and towns preaching about the kingdom (commonwealth) of God, with a message of reconciliation, forgiveness and healing. It was a simple plan. His activities continually drew large crowds wherever he went, including some of the religious leadership who had various reasons for wanting to hear him. It is abundantly clear that Jesus excited, inspired and challenged these crowds. The cumulative effect of his life and teaching created—and still creates—a liberating, uplifting, inviting, if demanding, feel to this wandering teacher. This quality is wonderfully captured by two of his disciples after they unknowingly meet the risen Jesus on the road to Emmaus, saying "didn't our hearts also burn while he was speaking to us." (Luke 24).

Jesus did not offer philosophical lectures. By means of engaging, pointed, parables, and bursts of ethical teachings he illustrated how one should live, what God wants and what God is like. He taught that God calls for righteous and just living, yet was also like a merciful father or mother yearning to be reunited and reconciled with his children.

There is great promise in Jesus' message, as well as a strong message about how to live in this life, how we should treat each other—truly a Way of life, which is no doubt why his followers soon after became known as people of the Way, for they were living in a different and compelling way, demonstrating their caring for one another and others.

A large part of what these religious leaders challenged Jesus about concerned his breaking of numerous religious laws (especially of the Sabbath), questioning him about what he was teaching and those he was associating with. A noteworthy observation is that, whereas Jesus was greatly forgiving of the crowds of the marginalized, the poor and sinners, he was frequently angry with many of the religious leaders. As we saw in the opening quotes, Jesus said that these leaders not only misunderstand the heart of the scriptures, they also caused the people to lose their way and miss the path of faithfulness to God. He exclaimed, "you make them twice as fit for Gehenna (hell)" (Matt 23:15). The changes Jesus was offering were major, even dramatic, and yet they are beautiful and life-giving and liberating. They are a part of the "truth that sets you free." Indeed, God does not require numerous religious acts and sacrifices, God requires simply and profoundly, a Way of love, as we see here:

> When Jesus accepted an invitation to eat in the house of a Pharisee, a woman of ill repute came in, weeping and anointing Jesus' feet with oil. A Pharisee was offended thinking "if this man were a prophet, he would have known what kind of woman this is who is touching him" (religiously unclean). Jesus responded with a simple story of two people, whose debts were cancelled. One debt had been small, the other large. Jesus asks, "which of them will love the creditor more?" Simon responds, "the one for whom he cancelled the greater debt." Jesus replied, "You have judged rightly. Then turning toward the woman he said to Simon, "Do you see this woman? I entered your house; you gave me no water for my feet, but she has bathed my feet with her tears and dried them with her hair. You gave me no kiss, but from the time she came in she has not stopped kissing my feet. You did not anoint my head with oil, but she anointed my feet with ointment. Therefore, I tell you, her sins, which are many, have been forgiven; hence she has shown great love. But to the one whom little is forgiven, loves little." Then he said to her, "Your sins are forgiven." (Luke 7: 36-50)

Leaving aside customs that are strange to us, is this not a beautiful and compelling story of forgiveness and love for the broken, despised, and lowly of this world, in contrast to the small-heartedness of the religious leader who put religious laws above mercy. That is why in another conflict with a religious leader, Jesus exclaimed, quoting Hosea 6:6, "Go and learn what this means, *I desire mercy, not sacrifice.*" Any person whom he encountered was a loved and valuable child of God to Jesus—he paid no heed to customs and regulations which said women and children should not come near, nor persons from other towns or ethnicities, nor persons with sicknesses attributed to sinfulness, or even individuals who were sinners. He looked deep into their eyes, spoke with them, forgave them, healed them. And this angered many.

In another moment, on a Sabbath day, Jesus' disciples were walking and very hungry. So they plucked heads of grain to eat and ate them. Here is what occurred: "The Pharisees said to him, "Look, why are they doing what is unlawful on the Sabbath?" And Jesus said to them, "Have you never read what David did when he and his companions were hungry and in need of food? He entered the house of God, when Abiathar was high priest, and ate the bread of the Presence, which is not lawful for any but the priests to eat, and he gave some to his companions. Then he said to them, "The Sabbath was made for humanity, not humanity for the Sabbath; so the Son of man is lord even of the Sabbath" (Mark 2:23ff).

Is this not a powerful, beautiful and revolutionary change in the meaning of religious?—or one could say, it is moving *beyond religion*. I will return to this last quote later, because of its importance. In all these episodes we feel the change, the radical new wine, of Jesus' teaching and example. He was elevating or transforming certain elements of the Jewish tradition in bold ways. Jesus makes clear that religion and being faithful are foremost about being merciful, compassionate and just, not fulfilling hundreds of laws and rituals.

I am calling this Jesus transformation beyond religion, noting that if people are leaving religion, I want to proclaim heartily and joyfully, that the heart of what Jesus proclaims connects with what many non-religious people also believe and endorse—that the way of fulfilling life is to live a life of bold love, unhampered by deadening laws and rituals. Jesus grounds this message in the revelation that God graciously loves, forgives, and accepts us as we are, setting us free to live and love joyfully! In the next chapter, and at different times in this book, I will jump forward to the present for the implications of Jesus' work.

Reflection Questions

1. Discuss your reactions to the tough proclamations of Jesus and the prophets in this chapter, and the conflict with some of the religious establishment.

Chapter 3. Living Jesus' Way

The message of Jesus and the prophets in their denunciations of religious ceremony and sacrifice is large, alive, and vocal
in modern times. Dr. Martin Luther King Jr. marched across the
country referencing the biblical prophets, as he called for justice
"to roll down like mighty waters," while some religious voices were
saying, "slow down, not now, don't be so disruptive." King was
fighting against mistreatment and inequality specifically for black
people, but he was clear that his efforts were for the poor, the persecuted, and those without power—ultimately his vision was for all
people as he declared that he was working for that day "when all
men (and women) could sit down together at the table of the Lord."

King's work was in harmony with Jesus' teachings, including the memorable parable in Matthew 25 that concludes with the
statement "As you did it unto the least of these, my brothers and
sisters, you did it unto me." Jesus invites all people, but shows a
special concern for the downtrodden, outcast, and marginalized.
Despite Dr. King's assassination 50 years ago, his legacy remains
powerful, and other prophetic voices are even now marching in the
name of the prophets, and of Jesus, demonstrating how following
Jesus connects with the work of justice. Yet quite a few who call
themselves Christian do not believe or understand how their faith
connects with justice, forgetting that the prophets often criticized
or challenged kings and religious leaders, and called them to es-
tablish justice in the land. They protest that the Christian message
is about reconciliation. Their protest is well intentioned, but they
miss the fullness of the message of reconciliation. Yes, we can celebrate the gift of our being reconciled to God through Christ, but
they forget that Jesus also called for reconciliation among peoples.
In the Sermon on the Mount, Jesus makes the pointed statement,
"So if you are offering your gift at the altar, and there remember

that your brother has something against you, leave your gift there before the altar and go; first be reconciled to your brother, and then come and offer your gift" (Matthew 5: 23-24). Reconciliation with your brother takes priority over your religious practice! This teaching seems too often neglected or forgotten.

To do this earthly aspect of reconciliation requires justice. Without it, reconciliation among people is hollow. This is critical to understand. Hollow reconciliation is one major reason many people have, and still do, turn away from religion. The struggling of the world protest, "Don't neglect and mistreat me now, and tell me I will get my pie in the sky later." Jesus did not do that. Rather, he kept declaring that how we treat others is a top priority, adding that on the Day of Judgment he will hold us to account on how we treated people, especially "the least of these, my brothers and sisters" (Matthew 25:31ff). The crucial call of reconciliation with justice is a pivotal component of the new wine for our time.

Jesus and the prophets' clash with empty religiosity harmonize, and at times it seems that Jesus raises it to another level. Earlier in the book I used only two of Jesus' "woe unto you religious leaders" denunciations in Matthew chapter 23—there are at least four more in that chapter, along with numerous other hard conflicts between Jesus and those leaders throughout all four gospels!

Jesus did not leave Judaism, but like the prophets, he condemned much of the religious practices of his day, declaring that the essence of the religious law is contained in two commandments: To love God with all your mind and heart, and to love your neighbor as yourself. If one *lives this Way*, one fulfills the religious law. Or, as he put it, "on these two commandments depend all the Law and the Prophets." Simple, profound, powerful, and liberating. He never says, "memorize the following creed, and in the time of judgment recite it, and you will enter the kingdom." Rather, he affirms those who are *doers* of the word. In Matthew 7:24-27 and

Luke 6:47-49 he offers a stern warning to those who hear the word but do not act in accordance.

In his parable referred to as the Pharisee and the Publican, we are told that Jesus directs it to "some who trusted in themselves that they were righteous and despised others." The righteous Pharisee prays, "God I thank thee that I am not like other men, extortioners, unjust, adulterers, or even this tax collector. I fast twice a week, I give tithes of all that I get. But the tax collector, standing far off , would not even lift up his eyes to heaven, but beat his breast, saying, "God, be merciful to me a sinner!" Jesus continues, "I tell you, this man went down to his house justified rather than the other." The Pharisee could be termed a religious star or exemplar, yet Jesus indicates that is of no value without a change of attitude, heart, and life.

We have seen that the extent and harshness of Jesus' conflict with the religious leaders is startling and even shocking. Although it takes place within Judaism, it is broader than that. Jesus alters the nature of religion to primarily a way of living, more than a practice of religious rituals, laws, and sacrifices. Though he does not call for the elimination of all forms or practices of religion, creating a large void, he taught that they must be a distant second to the call to love God and neighbor.

It is crucial to have communities that are caring, active, and faithful. These communities are the key vehicles where the faith is shared and taught, and the new life in God is nourished and emanates out into the world. There need to be some practices and ceremonies. But we need to be constantly vigilant, for history bears witness that this can lead down into the valley of hollow forms, neglecting what Jesus called "the weightier matters of the Law, justice, mercy and faith." Jesus jars people, freeing them from that road, while turning towards the "hard and narrow" road of love with its deep implications.

We see more of Jesus' transformation, the new wine, in his Sermon on the Mount. His series of declarations that begin, "you have heard that it was said. . . but I say to you . . ," taking older biblical teachings to another level, or even superseding them. Arguably, the most famous of those is "You have heard that it was said, 'An eye for an eye, and a tooth for a tooth.' But I say to you, do not resist an evildoer. But if anyone strikes you on the right cheek, turn the other also." (Matthew 5:38) I recall hearing that when Gandhi read this he remarked, "If we live by an 'eye for an eye,' then the whole world will be blind."

The prominent rabbi, Jonathan Sachs, concerning the *lex talionis*—the eye for an eye principle—said that people often miss a key feature of this rule. It invokes a sense of proportion in retaliation—it is *only* an eye for an eye. It attempts to prevent the escalation of violence and revenge. That is a significant point. But as Gandhi asserted, the world would still go blind. The tragedy of history is that as both individuals and nations practice eye-for-an-eye retaliation, retribution seems to never end. History also demonstrates that retaliatory responses often arise out of anger, pride and insult. These serve to escalate the punishment, destruction, and intimidation, with the attitude of "That'll teach 'em." The cycle of violence and war then continues. Someone or something has to break the cycle.

Another example is "You have heard that it was said, 'Love your neighbor and hate your enemy.' But I say to you, Love your enemies, and pray for those who persecute you, so that you may be children of your Father in heaven" (Matt 5:43-45). Though that is a great challenge for those who feel offended, it is the surest way out of the spiral of retaliation, violence, and hatred.

Does this ever happen? Gandhi and Dr. King are two towering examples. On a smaller scale, but quite compelling, here is an incident recently reported on the news. It is good to bear in mind how Jesus frequently praised non-Jews, and I am thinking of the Roman Centurion, when he said "Not even in all Israel have I seen such faith." The report was from a small town in the U.S. about an older man (not sure if he was Christian) who despised Muslims, and who posted many harsh statements about them on social media. A local Muslim town official noticed this and was disturbed. He wondered what he might do. He noticed that the angry man was saddled with significant medical debt. He decided to send a modest donation to help with the debt, and he posted it to his friends. They created a Go Fund Me account, resulting in enough money to enable the angry fellow to pay off the debt. He was so moved that he met with him and they became friends. Not long after, when his new Muslim friend was running for re-election, he insisted that he place one of his re-election signs on the his lawn. Reconciliation. Change of heart. Love of enemy. Cycle of violence ended, as a Muslim practices Jesus' teaching.

On the individual level, Jesus' ethic of love of enemy and forgiveness and mercy does break the cycle. That is not so easy on the nation level, to find a way that stops the endless life-for-life and bomb-for-bomb, and "you did this to us, so we must do so unto you" cycle of death.

I will not dive into explanations of all of Jesus' *but-I-say-unto-you* pronouncements, but those that I have discussed demonstrate that Jesus challenged or transformed much of the religious law and practice that had piled up over the centuries, such as the well over 600 Sabbath laws observed in the time of Jesus—for violations of which he was frequently called out.

The Pharisees and Sadducees who show up to hear Jesus throughout his ministry constantly question or challenge him. A few, like Nicodemus, are drawn to him, but it appears that the majority saw Jesus as a threat and a problem. The discussion of removing him continued throughout his ministry culminating in his Crucifixion. There we find another religion-altering moment. Matthew 27:51 reports that while hanging on the Cross, "Jesus cried with a loud voice and yielded up his spirit. And behold, the curtain of the temple was torn in two, from top to bottom; and the earth shook, and the rocks were split." The Curtain in the Temple that separated the Holy of Holies from the world, was opened and revealed to all. God is not locked up in the Temple any more. God is not possessed by buildings, nor religion, nor the religious class. Theologian Paul Tillich writes: "The curtain which made the temple a holy place, separated from other places, lost its separating power. . . . When the curtain of the temple was torn in two, God judged religion and rejected temples. After this moment temples and churches can only mean places of concentration on the holy which is the ground and the meaning of every place."[4]

This powerful moment is often missed if the reader thinks the event is simply a matter of earthquake damage. In another sermon called *The Yoke of Religion*, Tillich writes: "The burden He (Jesus) wants to take from us is the burden of religion. It is the yoke of the law, imposed on the people of His time by the religious teachers."[5]

Yet religion keeps reverting to laws and rituals. They multiply and grow with the vigor of weeds unchecked. They can frequently strangle the flowers and fruits of the essence of living a holy (loving) life, the type of life Jesus demonstrated and spoke about. The New Testament describes this Way of Jesus, this "truth that sets you free." Many people do not seem to think through what Jesus means when he says, "I am the way and the truth and the life." They believe it simply means that, when you say his name, out of the kiosk comes the salvation ticket. In a sense, there is a piece of the truth in that idea, but Jesus makes abundantly clear

4   Tillich, Paul. 2005. The new being. Lincoln: University of Nebraska Press., pp. 177-78
5   Tillich, Paul. *The Shaking of the Foundations*, 2011, p. 95

that it is how we treat others, along with worshipping God, that leads to the abundant life—a life abundant in love, joy fulfillment, etc. This is the eternal life that begins now. It begins when we start walking in his Way, what is also called following Jesus. If we walk with Jesus, even if we carry many perplexing questions or deep hurts or losses or failures, yet we are accepted by the God of love as pure gift (grace). Such is the truth that sets us free—free to live in bold love and in the awareness that God accepts us freely by grace (salvation!). We need not live in the fear that we will stumble, come up short, and be rejected. "There is no fear in love, but perfect love casts out fear." (1 John 4:18). Here we see again how a focus on Jesus is key to understanding our faith and informing our understanding of the scriptures.

Another poignant example of Jesus' challenge to religion as a comprehensive body of laws and traditions comes in the defining, opening two chapters of the short gospel of Mark. It's quick, repetitive structure, method, and conclusion emphasize importance. There is no birth story in Mark. John the Baptist opens it with the announcement that the Messiah is coming. In fact he points to Jesus and exclaims, "There He is." He baptizes Jesus, who then goes through his time of Temptations, calls his crew of disciples, and comes out swingin', jumping right in with his essential mission of teaching, forgiving, and healing. We immediately also see the beginning of his conflicts with religious leaders. The second chapter, after a series of brief conflicts, concludes with a pivotal pronouncement that I think many non-Jews don't adequately comprehend: "The Sabbath was made for man, and not man for the Sabbath" (Mark 2: 27). In Judaism the Sabbath is pivotal, of tremendous importance. Jesus had just broken one of the hundreds of Sabbath laws. Jesus' disciples were hungry, so they harvested a little food on the Sabbath and ate it, despite the injunction against working on the Sabbath. The Pharisees called him out on that, and he responded that the Sabbath is for the benefit of the people, for the purpose of human flourishing, not a religious burden and holy requirement. Jesus' follow-up comment on this matter was also simple and surprising: He asks the leaders, if one of your sheep falls in a ditch on the Sabbath, won't you pull it out? How is that for a theological discussion?

It is hard to overstate the significance of this Sabbath transformation. This was no misdemeanor, it was a felony. Jesus was pointing out that religion should enhance life and human flourishing, not restrict and stifle life. This is a defining declaration placed at the beginning of the gospel. Chapter three of Mark tells us that some of the religious and political leaders were already conspiring as to how to stop Jesus.

All the gospels follow Him in his ministry, in which Jesus frequently broke religious traditions and laws. Probably his most frequent transgression was his interactions with 'unclean' people, or outsiders, or women and children—people whom a true rabbi or prophet should avoid or keep at a distance. Jesus walked from town to town teaching about the commonwealth (kingdom) of God, frequently using incisive stories that we call parables, as well as healing and forgiving, saying that those two are nearly interchangeable! He was calling people to a Way of living, not to a set of intellectual assertions that gain you a ticket to heaven. He asserted that it is what you do and how you live that are most important. Jesus was so intent on demonstrating and teaching how we should live (or follow him), that he was not concerned when such things broke a religious law. His actions demonstrated and amplified his words. They fleshed out his teachings. Isn't that bold and beautiful?

That women frequently were in his company and sometimes traveled with him, startled, and even angered, some people—again, mostly the religious leaders, who strongly maintained that it was religiously wrong for him and his disciples to do so. Jesus simply did it. In Luke 8 we read "Jesus went through the cities and villages, proclaiming the good news of the kingdom of God. The twelve were with him, as well as many women. . . . "Mary Magdalene, Joanna, Susanna, *and many others*" (italics mine). People don't forget shocking actions. A modern reader might gloss over that, but it was a big deal for Jesus to include women as well as many others of low or unclean status, as well as people from other nations, even enemies. God's invitation and God's work is broad and inclusive.

In Jesus' time, people believed incorrectly that crippled or diseased people were that way because of their sin, yet Jesus healed and accepted them. When a tower collapsed and killed several people, he taught that they are no more sinful than any of us—another beautiful truth that sets us free.

By allowing contact with "an unclean woman of ill repute," Jesus rattled many religious leaders. He not only welcomed her, he forgave her because of the depth of her love. He criticized any religious leaders who focused on "outer cleanliness" when inwardly they were not clean. He interacted with others who were thought to be unclean or undeserving, such as lepers, sinners, tax collectors, outsiders, as well as children.

Jesus stepped it up to another level, saying not only "let the children come to me" but "unless you change and become like children, you will never enter the kingdom of heaven" (Matthew 18:3). In modern parlance we could say that Jesus was not playing with these religious leaders, as he spoke truth strongly, directly, and clearly.

He interacted with non-Jews, on several occasions praising them highly. After indicating that the greatest commandments are to love God and to love your neighbor as yourself, a lawyer asked him, "And who is my neighbor?" Jesus responded with one of his most famous parables—the Good Samaritan. In this parable an unknown person is robbed and beaten and left on the side of the road. The first two people to pass by the victim were religious leaders (a priest and a Levite). They do not help. A third person stops, a hated outsider (Samaritan) who, with great generosity, takes care of the bleeding victim. Jesus then asked the lawyer, "Which of these three, do you think, was a neighbor to this man who fell into the hands of the robbers?" The lawyer responded, "The one who showed him mercy." Jesus said to him, "Go and do likewise." This added to the anger of some of the religious leaders. His parables are not entertaining tales; they contain shocking elements, put the hearer on edge, pose a moment of decision, and reveal a new perception—more "new wine."

Reflection Questions

1. What are the two largest takeaways you have from this chapter?

2. Listen to responses from others, then discuss.

3. To what extent have you thought about Christianity in terms of justice and reconciliation? Discuss.

Chapter 4. The Power of Forgiveness and its Centrality

Healing and forgiveness were a large and central aspect of Jesus' life and mission. It is what he does time and again, sometimes indicating that the two are essentially the same. An example of this is when they lower a paralytic through an opening in the roof for Jesus to heal, and Jesus says to him "Your sins are forgiven." The scribes observing this were offended; maybe healing was okay, but what right did he have to forgive? Jesus responds by referring to himself as the "Son of Man," a messianic figure in the scriptures, who has authority. Even so, in what appears to be a concession to the scribes, Jesus turns to the paralytic and utters, "I say to you, rise, take up your pallet and go home." Jesus declares both healing with forgiveness.

I will add two rather dramatic examples to demonstrate the importance and magnificence of Jesus and forgiveness.

First I will take an episode in the gospel of John chapter 8, referred to as "A woman caught in adultery," though no mention was made of the man involved. The scribes and Pharisees brought her to Jesus where they asked him, "In the law Moses commanded us to stone such women. Now what do you say?" In a mysterious action, "Jesus bent down and wrote with his finger on the ground." We never find out what or why. But then, "When they kept on questioning him, he straightened up and said to them, "Let anyone among you who is without sin be the first to throw a stone. And once again he bent down and wrote on the ground. When they heard it, they went away, one by one, beginning with the elders. And Jesus was left alone with the woman standing before him."

"Jesus straightened up and said to her, "Woman, where are they? Has no one condemned you?" She said, "No one sir." And Jesus said, "Neither do I condemn you. Go your way and do not sin again." (John 8:1-12)

In this stunning and dangerous moment, it is evident that this is forgiveness—forgiveness and acceptance at a deep, life-changing level. It moves me every time I read or hear it. (It is beautifully portrayed in Franco Zefferelli's epic film *Jesus of Nazareth*).

Another, compelling example is Matthew 18: 21-22. In this quick interchange Peter comes to Jesus and asks, "Lord how often shall my brother sin against me, and I forgive him? As many as seven times? Jesus said to him, I do not say to you seven times, but seventy times seven." I am puzzled by biblical literalists, as I guess they need to keep long lists in which they keep track of each time various individuals act badly towards them. It must tax their patience waiting to get to 70 times 7, equaling 490 offenses! Rather, I think it is clear that Jesus, in his short, powerful style, is shocking Peter, and the listener, with the truth that forgiveness has no limits. We need to be as forgiving to others as God is forgiving to us. It is a key part of the Lord's Prayer, as it is at the core of the gospel—the Good News. So life changing can forgiveness be, we see that when Jesus healed people of physical or psychological ailments, he demonstrated that forgiveness and healing are nearly interchangeable. Consider also, that in New Testament Greek, the word for salvation also means to heal or make whole. It also contains the element of letting go. When we forgive, we let go of such things as anger, hate, and revenge, thus freeing our spirit and sometimes even physical symptoms, as well as offering to the other person the opportunity to be freed of them as well. When this occurs in its fullness, one experiences a foretaste of salvation.

Adding to the demonstration of forgiveness as the very heart of the Good News, there is the overarching moment when Jesus was on the Cross. Though beaten, mocked, and bleeding, he utters the words, "Father forgive them for they know not what they do," wrapping his whole life in the blanket of forgiveness. Jesus does not call for God's wrath on all those who rejected, persecuted, and mistreated him. "Father forgive them."

In the parable of The Prodigal Son, we hear a compelling and heart-changing story of a father (God) who yearns for his lost son and who is forgiving and loving without calculation or limit. His younger son, earlier than appropriate, asks for his inheritance. He goes off and lives a wild and reckless life and soon hits bottom. He decides to return to his father begging for mercy, even to be just a hired servant. He prepares his confession, expecting to be scolded and to be put out to work with the pigs. Before he even gets to his home, his father comes running down the road, embraces him, ignoring and cutting off his confession, and calls for a major feast, saying "For this my son was dead, and is alive again. He was lost, and is found." No punishment—rather, welcome and celebration. So shocking is this that the older, obedient son who is working hard in the fields, is angered and stays away in protest. The father does not come out yelling and waving his finger at the older son, but rather speaks these unforgettable words in Luke 15: "Son, you are always with me, and all that is mine is yours. But we had to celebrate and rejoice, because this *brother of yours* was dead, and has come to life; he was lost and has been found." (Italics mine)

With those words we see Jesus teaching that God not only forgives the wayward son, He also reaches out and affirms the obedient son. God runs out to welcome the lost child, and then God also works to restore the relationship between the brothers! Thus, this is a parable of forgiveness as well as restoring relationships— reconciliation between father (God) and son, and reconciliation between sons. Moving beyond patriarchy, we know it is between God and persons, and person to person. This is a central portrayal of both the Good News (gospel) and also of what God is like according to Jesus. That is why I believe this parable could also be called the Parable of the Amazing Father. Some have even referred to this parable as "the gospel within the gospel." Countless books and millions of sermons since then, if the message is faithful to the story, have transformed hearts and drawn people towards God and towards each other.

Jesus' good news is a deeply fulfilling, sometimes difficult, way of living. It is a true Way of Love, that sets us free from the mud of religion, and sends us out into the world with the power of love and the message of reconciliation. Paul says in II Corinthians that we are "ambassadors for Christ." Perhaps I should have new business cards, stating, *Ambassador for Christ.*

Yet I dare say that, in some regards, I agree with the growing crowd of people who have turned from religion. So much of it seems troubled or diseased. But for those people, to those people, I present this life-fulfilling message and the wonderful Jesus Way of Life, unfettered from religious trivia, condemnation, holy war, escapism, and other paraphernalia. Don't throw Jesus out with the ugly aspects of religion. Look for love, for there is where you find God. A way of love is not simplistic, absolutely not trivial. It is heart-opening, it is liberating, it is fulfilling and enduring.

One cannot speak of the Good News without a brief reflection on joy, for Jesus tells us that he came so that we might have joy (John 15:11), though adding the seeming paradox that "the way is hard and the way is narrow that leads to life." While joy and happiness may overlap, for me joy is more transcendent and meaningful. I found great happiness in playing basketball for close to four decades, and am grateful for it. It was a significant part of my life. But when I think of joy, I think of moments when I am able to do or participate in something meaningful, helpful, uplifting for a family member, a friend, or a stranger in need, or advocating and organizing for the many poor in my city of Philadelphia, or helping to create an impactful outreach or education program. Such endeavors are not always pleasure-filled, but they endure and bring a joy into life that lasts a lifetime. Deep in my being I know and feel that, by helping any of God's children (all people), you do something wonderful and enduring—"three things endure, faith, hope and love. But the greatest of these is love." (I Corinthians 13:13). I have observed uncountable instances where it is clear that people find great joy in helping people in need. Yes, the discipleship road is hard, but joy springs forth over and over again.

I think of the phrase in Psalms, "Joy comes in the morning." The magnificence of nature and also of music brings me both happiness and joy. Joy is part of the journey in Jesus' Way of life.

Some nonreligious people surely say, "I have had such joyful experiences and I don't believe in God." Hopefully all people have joy in their lives. But it moves us to another hard question. Traditionally, the Christian tradition stated that a person might have good fortune or joy in this life, but if they did not assent to the essential doctrines of faith, they were going to hell. Jesus gave a dramatic response that many Christians don't seem to fully grasp. In his parable of the last Judgment in Matthew 25 he states this about some people who may not have acknowledged him, so that in the Judgment they say to Jesus, "When did we see you hungry, or naked, or in prison, or sick and helped you," and I will say to them, "Enter the kingdom which is prepared for you because as you did it unto the least of these my brothers and sisters, you did it unto me." Enter the kingdom of heaven! Multiple times Jesus taught that it is the doers of the word who are on the right road, even if they don't realize it. It becomes clear that there are people outside Christianity who are following Jesus' Way—and He will welcome them. They too find joy on this road.

I have been reading and studying the Bible for five decades. And one day, around the age of 60, I read a passage that I know I had read before, but when I read it this time, I was blown away. In the first letter of John—1John 4:7ff—it states "Everyone who loves is born of God and knows God. Whoever does not love does not know God, for God is love." Several verses later it says, "God is love, and those who abide in love abide in God, and God abides in them." I can almost hear loud voices protesting and quoting other scriptures. Despite the potential for endless arguments, divisiveness, and conflict, this simple gospel fits with Jesus' profound depth and simplicity, even as he summed up the Law and the Prophets, "Love God with all your heart, and love your neighbor as yourself." (as Paul does also!) The Way of Jesus really is a Way of Love.

Reflection Questions:

1. What are your thoughts about the extent and harshness of Jesus' conflict with many of the religious leaders of his day?—culminating in his statement "The Sabbath was made for man, not man for the Sabbath."

2. Have you encountered religion that is in conflict with Jesus' teaching and Way? Share such examples.

3. How does or can your faith community engage this Jesus transformation?

Chapter 5. The Path of Discipleship

With the liberating and joyful Good News described in the earlier chapters, Jesus called out his followers to a life of "faith working through love" (Galatians 5:6). It is a rugged road of witness, worship, reconciliation, justice and mercy, understood as compassionate service. All of these are fruits of Love. I propose four main categories for this path of discipleship:

1) Communities of love
2) Sharing the Good News and worship
3) The mission of reconciliation and justice
4) The works of compassion and charity

Like tables and chairs, for stability and strength, all four components are needed in the path of discipleship.

Communities of Love

Following Jesus needs to be supported by a community of loving disciples. Yes, there is a personal dimension to faith, a personal decision to follow him. But even when Jesus walked the earth, they followed him in a group (made up of disciples and usually a company of women as well). Communities of love (churches) are the soil from which the fruits of the gospel grow. Jesus wanted the mark of those called out—the church—to be love. It should be strong and obvious, causing people to say "See those Christians how they love another." Certainly the love will flow outward, but the family of God is the incubator, a place of much love. This, indeed, happened in the early, persecuted church in the Roman Empire, yet the church spread and grew mightily. The examples of these new communities was so compelling in the first century that the book of Acts (account of the early church) mentions at least 4 times that these Jesus followers were being called people of "The Way." They were sharing all they had and caring for others beyond their community, undaunted by adversity.

A genuinely loving community is a permanent, necessary base of discipleship. Given the necessity of such community, we will always need to be working on the health of the community. We are human—there will always be conflict, ego, eruptions of selfishness, and so forth. As much as possible we should try to work through this, to heal the wounds, to forgive and accept forgiveness. This is ongoing, sometimes difficult work. Let's do it—we are the family of God. This also requires being generous in our embrace of other faith communities as fellow members of the greater family.

As part of several congregations, and familiar with quite a few others, I have observed that they are all caring communities, imperfect as they might be. I have never found a church anywhere that does not care for its members and also help those in need. The sum total of all that caring is vast, though not often making headlines. Of course, making headlines is not the purpose of good works, but the abundance of good works of faith communities should be noted, not just the scandals and divisions. The good works are constant. As I write in the time leading to Christmas, stories of generosity, kindness and love are endless. One recent news story was about a church successfully raising money to relieve an impoverished person buried in medical debt! These deeds continue year round through the church. There are also groups of people, some of faith and others not, marching and advocating for greater justice for the poor and addressing ongoing racism. Throughout a growing number of faith communities there is a powerful call to serve others in charity, compassion, justice, and reconciliation.

The church that I have worshipped in over the last three decades has been a wonderful and faithful example, despite our human imperfections. They have striven for decades for what we call "the inner—outer journey," meaning the need for prayer, contemplation, and worship coupled with deep involvement, service, and action in the world. The inner journey is the place to pray and center, the place to discern what one is called out to do, the place to renew and find strength and inspiration, and the place of perpetual return.

Worship and Sharing the Good News

Worshipping and sharing the Good News is a vitally important part of the mission of these communities. With the Good News of the gospel, *this treasure* as Paul calls it, it follows that we want to share it. We share it in worship to rejoice, remind us, and re-energize ourselves for this mission. Years ago my wife, who is a nurse, was working in a hospital in Trenton, New Jersey. She was talking with an African-American nursing colleague, and at one point she said to my wife, "What do you do to get happy in church?" That really struck me. The world can be a very difficult and unfair place, so this woman's church provides a refuge, a place to rejoice and renew, and then to return to the challenges of life. It is much more than an escape for an hour or two, but also a source of recharging, finding the joy of which Jesus spoke, and the strength to "keep on keeping on."

Some churches bring more restrictions, rigidity, and religiosity to worship than is needed. I suspect that Jesus would likely reprimand such practices, as he did to religious leaders in his day, and I suggest that it is nicely proposed in a one-liner from Jesus to a Pharisee, quoting the prophet Hosea, "Go and learn what this means, I desire mercy, not sacrifice."

Hearing the good news in church, we equip ourselves to share it outside the church. Opportunities arise in day-to-day life for offering our message, or sharing excitedly about some service or ministry that we are involved in. At an opportune moment we might add, "I do these things because I believe they are the right and just things to do, as well as what my faith calls me to do."

Jesus called for "doers of the word," and it is still often true that actions speak more powerfully than words. And your words can be few! Parts three and four are all about Doing the word. While in prison, John the Baptist apparently had fallen into some doubt about Jesus, because he sent someone to Jesus to ask, "Are you the One, or should we look for another?" Jesus responded, "Go back and report to John what you have seen and heard: The blind receive sight, the lame walk, those who have leprosy are cleansed, the deaf hear, the dead are raised, and the good news is proclaimed to the poor." (Luke 7:22) Jesus doesn't say yes, just "tell him what you see and hear"—his deeds provide the answer.

Loving communities are not new, but sometimes their forms or practices need to evolve. The parts of worship and the music may vary. Generally, I believe this is good. Great efforts and creativity should be aimed to attract those who have left organized religion—the skeptical, agnostic, suspicious, wounded, etc. They need to be drawn by bold, new wineskins

Recognizing the need for new wineskins, within the Presbyterian church, new initiatives and ministries have been launched, including Next Church, Matthew 25 churches, and Vital Congregations. They require a deep preparation of prayer, reflection, assessment, and commitment.

I see numerous newer independent churches, which I discovered we should not be too quick to dismiss. In my neighborhood, a new church started about two years ago, and I finally visited it. I was pleasantly surprised. It seemed to me to be a good and faithful church. It was being held in a local high school auditorium. I walked in to find a truly integrated congregation (how often does that happen?), and saw people of all ages, singing modern hymns and music. The sermon on loving our neighbors was excellent. It was wonderful to see praise, joy, and outreach. During announcements they spoke of a huge upcoming outreach to special needs children from all around Philadelphia. Beautiful—by their fruits you shall know them! Just minutes from my home I found a dynamic new wineskin.

This does not dismiss the well-known terrible fruit— massive sex scandals, cover-ups, misuse of church funds, hatred towards groups of people, and narrow-minded rejection of other perspectives. All the more reason why in our times, we need to be big on our actions of love and reconciliation and thoughtful in our declarations.

The Works of Compassion and Charity

With the millions of churches worldwide, there are few, if any, that do not help and share with those in need. In the United States this reaches a tremendous climax during Thanksgiving and Christmas, though it certainly goes on all year round. Church-based efforts are frequently joined by many other organizations and individuals outside faith communities, multiplying the scale and effectiveness of these programs. The total giving of church communities is very large indeed. As Chair of the Outreach committee in our church, I coordinate our work and support for many fine missions and services, both near and far. We also have an additional goal. For nearly all of our local outreach, we have people from the church directly involved. We don't simply write checks. We believe in the importance of direct involvement. Thankfully, other faith communities are also deeply involved. It is uplifting to witness the vast amount of volunteering and service. For all the compassion spread through charity, we are aware and do not ignore criticisms about the limits—even dangers—of charity, such as those addressed in the book *Toxic Charity*. Charity by itself usually does not help bring people to self-development, self-sufficiency, and dignity. Of course, there are many situations where immediate charity is needed. All told, we cannot neglect the works of justice and reconciliation, which is part 4.

The Work of Reconciliation and Justice

While reconciliation is the very heart of Christianity, justice and reconciliation are like a left and right shoe, you can't get far without a complete pair. It is critical to raise up and increase the work of both, and to keep them connected. Both ideas are deeply imbedded in the biblical narrative. Today we must ask, what should they look like now? That itself is a very biblical idea: we repeatedly hear God saying "Behold I am doing a new thing." (Isaiah 43), and continuing through to the book of Revelation which declares that ultimately God will make all things new again.

The core of the gospel is about God reconciling the world to God's self, followed by reconciliation between Jews and Gentiles, meaning among all peoples of the earth. Returning again to the parable of the Prodigal Son, as the example par excellence, in portraying an image of God expressing joy, forgiveness, and generosity when reconciling a lost son, and then going further to reconcile brother to brother, and person to person. To a person who is not religious, or has left or rejects religion, I offer this parable as one that illustrates God's desire to be in loving relationship with us, and who also wants us to be in loving relationship with each other, which is reconciliation. Bringing people together, and also into relationship with God, is the heart and soul of Christianity. I believe most people would like to live in a reconciled world.

It can be said that the whole biblical saga is about reconciliation, with profound implications for out time. Paul reminded the early followers, that, having been reconciled to God, God has "given us the ministry of reconciliation" (II Corinthians:5:18). Jesus taught that reconciliation with God is tied to our reconciling with others, harmonizing perfectly with what Jesus called the Great Commandments: "You shall love God with all your heart and strength, and you shall love your neighbor as yourself, on these two depend all the Law and the Prophets."

Therefore, in the discussion of reconciliation we are touching upon the essence of what it means to follow Jesus. I take us now to a hidden gem—two verses from the Sermon on the Mount. I call it hidden because, until the recent day when I visited Epic church, I do not recall ever hearing a sermon directly on these two verses, which are in Jesus' Sermon on the Mount: "So when you are offering your gift at the altar, if you remember that your brother or sister has something against you, leave your gift there before the altar and go; first be reconciled to your brother or sister, and then come and offer your gift." (Matthew 5:23-24)

This instruction is religiously transformative. It is a direct and poignant teaching that reconciliation of human relationships takes precedence over religious ritual and practice. It is not hard to interpret, though it posed a startling challenge to the religious establishment in Jesus' time, as well as our own. It is a divine challenge to the churches in all times and places—to give reconciliation among peoples precedence over religious rituals and the temptation to stay comfortably in our little churches and communities. Because the call to reconciliation is so central to the Good News, we must take a deeper dive into it.

I paraphrase those two verses as: "Put your religious practice on the back burner, and first get busy reconciling with your brothers and sisters." That is a big and holy task, but first we should look to our neighborhoods and our country. In our own country this includes, probably at the top of the list, opposing and removing the racism that still haunts us on the personal and structural levels. That's a tall order. Jesus made it a top priority. Speaking tough love again, Jesus, along with the Prophets, declared that God does not want to hear all the praising and preaching in church if we are not also at work in the world on being reconciled with our brothers and sisters! This call is above and beyond all that religious ritual that we might practice!

Jesus returns to this teaching multiple times, such as when he indicated that you can perform your detailed religious practices, but without "neglecting the weightier matters of justice, mercy and faith." (Matt 23:23). Pause and ponder Jesus' challenge. Jesus did not say to close down temples (though he just about did so in the famous episode in which he turned over tables in the temple). He pushed further in other declarations, denouncing religious dress and pageantry, rituals and pomp and circumstance, long, windy prayers—instead of heeding the prophetic call to justice and the wide call to reconciliation with God and people.

So much of what we see in the gospels is Jesus out in the world, in the streets, teaching, healing, sharing dinners, shaking up the religious establishment, hanging out with every sort of person, and in the process breaking many religious laws. Can we believe that Jesus would be fine if we say, "Listen, each year we go into poor neighborhoods, bring food and presents, Christmas greetings, sing carols together. Everybody is happy, and we offer prayers that the poor and outcast will find better days ahead," and then return to our separateness, enjoying our benefits within an unequal and unjust society. In the gospels, we do not see Jesus espousing such a message. Quite a few people profoundly abuse Jesus' saying about "the poor you have always with you," to justify a life of occasional charity. That statement regarding the poor was spoken in an exceptional moment in Jesus' journey, as he was nearing his Crucifixion—not a major guideline for the life of faith. It must not lead to the belief that having a large, poor population is acceptable, or even God's will. Occasional charity comes up very short in the call to love and to care for the broken, the poor, the ostracized, the marginal, the persecuted. We cannot neglect justice and reconciliation—they are the higher call.

The biblical God, as Jesus taught, is a God of justice. This is dramatically demonstrated in the story of the Exodus. Listen to these words from God as he spoke to Moses: "Then the Lord said, "I have seen the affliction of my people who are in Egypt, and have heard their cry because of their taskmasters; I know their sufferings, and I have come to deliver them." (Exodus 3:7-8)

All biblically grounded faith communities hold up this epic story, but how many let it lift them up and move them out into the world with the message, as Martin Luther King Jr. did? That was half a century ago. Now, too many faith communities, by their inaction, effectively do not see justice as an integral part of God's message and work in the world. It is good to see the present Pope and other denominational faith leaders making prophetic statements and pushing this cause, but generally this has not moved the majority of local churches and the millions of everyday parishioners into the deep waters of justice. Many Christians and Jews see God as caring for them, as well as calling for acts of kindness and generosity to the less fortunate, but little concerned with the call of justice and equality—which are a foundation for reconciliation. If we believe that all people are created in the image of God, then all people have dignity and all are equal. These truths require justice for all. In Dr. King's famous *I Have a Dream* speech, he speaks of the time "when all people will sit down at the table of the Lord, black and white, rich and poor, Protestant and Catholic and Jew, southerners with northerners"—enunciating the dream of reconciliation among all of God's children.

Indeed, let the compassionate work of charity continue, but we must do some careful homework and avoid offering only aspirin and band-aid measures for serious wounds and ailments, allowing these problems, these indignities, these inequalities, these wounds and diseases, to remain and fester. Love demands more than charity without justice, even as you and I would demand more if it were our family or friends who are suffering. Justice and love are connected. As Cornell West said, "Justice is what love looks like in public."

We cannot let justice be ignored denying numerous poor folk a living wage, well-funded schools, adequate housing—such basics as would provide for a decent life and human dignity. We must work for equality, change unfair policies, provide quality education that will enable people to rise out of poverty. Recently, a fine Christian colleague in my volunteer justice work, became agitated, explaining that many people don't understand that most poor folk don't want to depend on charity or government assistance to get by. They would rather receive a living wage that would enable them to support themselves and live decently! Neglect the work of advocacy and justice, and we keep people in perpetual poverty, dependency, and inequality, and diminish their dignity. With adequate wages and benefits, they would love not to depend upon soup kitchens, clothing handouts, rent assistance, and so on. Work has dignity, and gives dignity. It is an outrage to designate certain work of such little value that we will pay a wage that leaves people in squalor and desperation. The work of justice aims to change these realities. I cannot say strongly enough that this work is about human dignity, which is grounded in the truth that we are all created in the image of God! Let that guide our prayers and actions.

Inequality and poverty hurt too many people, and they require that we face the additional fact that they disproportionately affect people of color. As Dr. King said 50 years ago, we still have not lived up to our Declaration that states that "all men are created equal." Yet at our Founding, there was a great contradiction—only white male land-owning aristocrats had full rights, leaving out slaves as well as women, and claiming slaves were three-fifths of a person. This horrible contradiction is what author Jim Wallis and others have called the Original Sin of the United States. Though some people do not want to deal with these issues—in the pursuit of truth, dignity, and our faith, we must do so.

I have presented considerable biblical support demonstrating that God is angry about injustice, calling us to "do justice, love mercy, and walk humbly with God," within a wide loving embrace, and with justice emanating from this love. We dare not neglect the pursuit of justice for all.

A stunning and faith-informed example of the work of justice and reconciliation was the work in South Africa in the 1990s of the Truth and Reconciliation Commission. It began with the hard work of exposing the hurt and the crimes and listening to those who were harmed and oppressed speak their difficult truths. Then followed the work of reconciliation, rather than the usual historical reaction of revenge. Isn't this incredible? The native peoples of South Africa might have swept brutally across the country, taking back their land, beating, killing, or chasing out the descendants of colonialism. In a few cases that did happen. That Nelson Mandela, imprisoned for 27 years, one would think he would be filled with rage and vengeance. Yet this man of faith instead endorsed the Truth and Reconciliation Commission. The fact that South Africa still suffers with poverty and political challenges does not take away this historical movement that turned away from eye-for-an-eye retaliation and towards a deep process of genuine reconciliation.

In the United States, many of us wanted to believe that racism was dealt with in the Civil Rights movement of the 60's and that we have progressed far down the road toward ending racism. But the last few years have revealed that a dangerous reality of hatred and racism is still alive.

Additionally, there has been an explosion of recent historical research into what was done to African-Americans over the 400 years since the first slaves were brought to the United States in the early 1600s. Most have learned, somewhat briefly, about slavery in the first 250 years. Then President Lincoln takes us through the

Civil War and freed the slaves. If we thought of it much, we at least were relieved that it was something of the past—more than 100 years ago. However, much ugly information is being unearthed about the century of Jim Crow following Emancipation. Lawyer Bryan Stevenson has completed a massive documentation of over 4000 lynchings in that time—and recently helped dedicate a new museum on this research. That is why he calls the Jim Crow era an "Age of Terrorism."

These horrors led to great migrations of poor black people to the north—roughly six million people—who were then funneled into segregated, distressed neighborhoods. In this we see the creation of impoverished ghettoes in the north. Redlining helped maintain segregation. Additional research has uncovered how the war on drugs in the 1980s and '90s was used to incarcerate millions of young black men, creating the school-to-prison pipeline, which has also perpetuated the cycle of poverty. This ongoing research is filling in the vastly underreported history of those who suffered. Eye-opening books like *The New Jim Crow* by Michelle Alexander carefully documents what started in the 1980s under the slogan of the War on Drugs. Alexander's bestseller is a must read.

Everyone ought to know about the work, legal accomplishments, and writing of Bryan Stevenson. He has argued hundreds of cases at all levels, including five cases before the U.S. Supreme Court. Stevenson wrote a bestseller entitled *Just Mercy*. He has brought about significant change on both the state and national level. I strongly urge you to explore the website of The Equal Justice Initiative (5), for Stevenson's vast accomplishments and ongoing work. Bishop Desmond Tutu of South Africa has called him the Nelson Mandela of the United States. His large body of work informs and connects to what people of faith should be involved with, because it is the just thing to do and because it supports the work of reconciliation among all of God's people. This emerging surge for equality, justice and the end of racism is part of God's new wine for this time. It should be a key component of the new wineskins. Our communities of faith should strengthen us as we go out into the world with the message of reconciliation.

It is worth mentioning that in the weeks preceding the time I am writing this in 2019, it was uncovered that 300 Philadelphia police officers had shared racist comments on social media! And yet there are still people who think racism is all but gone, a thing of the distant past.

It is encouraging to note that there have been powerful examples of efforts at reconciliation from both races. I am particularly moved when African-Americans do so, given the history of the past 400 years. One of the most stunning moments occurred in 2013 by the response of church people from an African-American church in Charleston, South Carolina. After a troubled and hate-driven young white man came into a Bible study in their church and gunned down 9 people, people from that church stepped forward to offer forgiveness to the killer. Words can barely do justice to such an action. I wonder what went on in the minds of the whole nation as they witnessed this act of forgiveness on national television. This is in stark contrast to what we often have seen on television with many murder cases, in which loved ones or friends of the deceased want "justice"— punitive justice that wants the harshest possible punishment for the killer, sometimes adding the words, "I hope they rot in hell." The church people in Charleston broke the violent cycle of revenge in human history and the prevalence of "an eye for an eye" mentality. They said, "We forgive him." This does not mean that the killer should not be punished, yet their response is worlds apart from vengeance.

Here is an incident that I witnessed years ago, when I was driving a New York City cab during the summer before my senior year in Brooklyn College. It took place on 14th street in Manhattan, not far from Union Square, and did not make it into the news. There was a double-parked truck on the other side of the street from me with a white man at the steering wheel. The truck was blocking traffic in a very busy and jammed street. The truck driver was probably in his early fifties. In a car behind the truck waiting to proceed (along with a long line of other cars), there was an African-American man, perhaps in his 30s. They were shouting at each other, and it was getting heated, though with the surrounding horns honking and other noise, my windows closed with the air conditioner on, I could not hear what they were saying. The African-American man got out of his car and was walking to the truck. Seeing this, the white man grabbed a small pipe from inside his truck console and raised it. Mind you, this is moving quickly. The black man, who was fairly big, moved fast and jumped up on the side step to the truck, as the white man attempted to open the door. Then the black man was able to reach in and yank the pipe from his hand. I recall thinking, "This is going to get real bad." There would be no match between the older white man and the younger, larger black man, especially having wrested the pipe from the white man. This happened in a matter of seconds. Then, the black man lowered his hand with the pipe to his side, said a few words to the white man (I could not hear it), and walked away. The white man had brought the pipe into the conflict, and thank goodness (God?) the black man did not choose to use it, cutting off the cycle of violence. It was the early 1970s. Despite centuries of mistreatment, and all the racial conflict in the 1960s, I marvel that this black man did not strike a single blow. There was no violence. This incident did not make the news. A dangerous and dramatic moment where conflict and anger did not lead to violence and bloodshed, and did not make the news—yet decades later is now revealed.

Some people say that justice is not their 'thing' and prefer the works of charity, and get tired or upset with so much discussion of justice. Consider the following. About 2700 years ago in the nation of Israel there emerged a series of very remarkable individuals, whom we call the prophets. This happens several hundred years after the composing of the Torah, or foundation of Jewish faith. They are a strange crew, and they pop up in both the northern and southern kingdoms of Israel at various times over the course of a few centuries. Israel, like most nations, was religious. The nations prayed to their gods. They sang, praised, offered gifts, and sacrifice. The gods needed to be appeased. This was the center of their religiosity. The Hebrew prophets burst on the scene and attack what they see going on. They are outraged by unrighteousness and by injustice great and small, by dishonesty, violence, deceit, the neglect and mistreatment of the poor and vulnerable, and priests who are false. In his seminal book on the prophets, scholar and Rabbi Abraham Heschel writes: "The prophet knew that religion could distort what the Lord demanded of man, that priests themselves had committed perjury by bearing false witness, condoning violence, tolerating hatred, calling for ceremonies instead of bursting forth with wrath and indignation at cruelty, deceit, idolatry and violence.

"To the people, religion was Temple, priesthood, incense: "This is the Temple of the Lord, the Temple of the Lord, the Temple of the Lord" (Jer 7:4). Such piety Jeremiah brands as fraud and illusion. "Behold you trust in deceptive words to no avail" (Jer 7:8). Worship preceded or followed by evil acts is an absurdity. The holy place is doomed when people indulge in unholy deeds.

Jeremiah continues, "Will you steal, murder, commit adultery, swear falsely, burn incense to Baal, and go after other gods that you have not known, and then come and stand before Me in this house, which is called by My name, and say 'We are delivered!'— only to go on doing these abominations? Has this house, which is called by My name, become a den of robbers in your eyes?" [6]

6   Heschel, Abraham Joshua. The Prophets, Vol.1 New York: Harper Torchbooks, 1969, p. 11.

In this impressive book of 500+ pages entitled *The Prophets*, Heschel goes on to describe in detail and depth the astonishing messages of these prophets. Read just the first fifty or hundred pages of Heschel's book and you will be astonished. And when we turn to Jesus, we can see repeatedly that Jesus refers to and builds on the prophets. As I earlier stated, in the gospel of Luke Jesus launches his ministry with a reading from the prophet Isaiah, and echoes many of the messages of the prophets throughout his teachings—including his turning over of the money-changing tables in the Temple and crying out with the words from Jeremiah, "My house shall be called a house of prayer, but you have made it a den of robbers." But from the end of the age of the prophets before Jesus until the 20th century, the prophetic call for justice has hardly been raised up (though no doubt some of those who fought against slavery were prophetic in action, if not in speech). Christianity and Judaism have always tried to offer assistance to the poor, but that is only a piece of the prophetic message. Offering assistance does not address the key theme of justice in the prophets.

However, the full prophetic message was clearly raised up by Dr. Martin Luther King, Jr. (it is not surprising that Heschel walked in the frontlines with King!). I certainly believe and maintain that we must always be asking how or what God and the gospels are calling us to do in our times—new wine. At this time, with nearly 8 billion people, great poverty, oppression, racism and inequality, God's prophetic message is more important than ever! Random acts of kindness are nice, but the God of the Bible and of Jesus will not settle for ignoring all the injustice. If we truly care for "the least of these," as Jesus called them, then we dare not neglect justice. It is a greater call than charity. Justice may never be perfect in human history, but each victory can raise up some of God's children. Justice is love that seeks to create the conditions for all people to be able to live a decent life and therefore to live with the dignity of everyone being a child of God. Surely you and I want this, and may well be among those who have even more than we need! Don't our hearts feel and move us to want to reduce human suffering and erase human indignity? Don't we know the truth of the prophet Jeremiah quoted above, that God rejects us saying, "We have the Temple (Church)" without the practices of love, of reconciliation, and justice. The prophet Micah also declares that God has no interest in sacrifices, of offerings of gold and silver and rivers of oil. Micah concludes his denunciations of ritual worship with the religion-transforming words: God "has showed you what is good; and what does the Lord require of you but to do justice, love mercy, and walking humbly with God" (Micah 6:8). Aware of this prophetic call or not, many faith communities have either lost this awareness or choose not to follow it.

Reflection Questions

1. When have you or your faith community deeply discussed the central call of Reconciliation, applying it concretely to the present moment in our communities and beyond? In any event, have this discussion now.

2. Discuss the theme that reconciliation and justice are deeply connected. Include the contradiction of trying to reconcile with people while ignoring deep inequality or injustice.

Chapter 6. Tastes of New Wine

Authors like Diana Butler-Bass in her book *Christianity After Religion* and Jim Wallis in *The Great Awakening*, assert that we are in a new Awakening as well as being some of the architects of this new wine. Various churches and denominations are spawning new creative ministries. I have been involved with Broad Street Ministry within the Presbytery of Philadelphia. Broad Street Ministry (BSM) started in 2005 in a once-prosperous downtown church that had dwindled with the exodus of people to the suburbs until it closed. Philadelphia, like so many cities, has quite a few homeless in or near the downtown area. A talented young minister, Bill Golderer, had a vision of a new ministry to the homeless in this abandoned church. Others liked the vision, and the Presbytery said, "Let's do it!" It started with a few services like offering a couple of meals a week, giving out clothing and toiletries, etc. Many churches as well as the downtown business community liked what they saw, so more support started to come in. It has grown considerably. BSM has added medical services, art therapy, creative performances, support to people coming out of prison, and a place to receive mail for over 3,000 poor and mostly homeless folk—(I had never given thought to how vital being able to receive mail is for all of us, but especially for someone who is homeless)—a worship service on Sunday afternoon, and more. The business community continues to respond with help.

Hundreds, if not thousands, of volunteers assist with the range of services at BSM. The meal service component reaches out with a philosophy of Radical Hospitalty, welcoming anyone and treating each person with dignity, with a host greeting each person as a valued guest in a restaurant. The sanctuary no longer has pews, so it can be set up in many formats. For the meal, round tables are arranged attractively, covered, set up, and waiting for the guests. The wait staff, servers, and bussers are volunteers. Music is playing; there is no rush. During slower moments we are encouraged to sit down at a table and talk with those who have come. They are treated with the dignity that all God's children deserve. Before the meal, announcements are made about the various other services available each day—A true refuge, a sanctuary, a welcoming place.

We read in the gospels how Jesus frequently ate meals with those who were outsiders, or who were thought to be unclean. Table fellowship. So on both levels of the church, each day, hundreds of homeless, and many volunteers and staff, move about together as equals—as the children of God, meeting needs. BSM has heart and soul. Here is the church re-emerging with new wineskins of compassion and justice.

A brief sweep of historical developments leading up to the civil rights movement is instructive. In the United States in the 18th and 19th centuries people of faith emerged, calling for equality and justice for all. It was becoming apparent to many that slavery was wrong. Quaker John Woolman felt this call in the 1700s, and he traveled around the country with this message. Some of the Founding Fathers knew slavery was wrong, but they caved to the economic interests of the slave states and thereby contradicted the stated intent of this bold, new experiment. In the 19th century, the call of abolitionists grew. Often given little recognition, there also arose courageous women of faith calling for the equality of women, or at least the right to vote. With or without religious language, people were rising up and speaking out. Other voices were speaking out, such as Richard Allen, founder of the AME church, Frederick Douglas, Sojourner Truth, and Lucretia Mott. The small sect of Quakerism had a noteworthy number of such prophets. (For an excellent presentation of notable Quaker women's involvement for equality and the right to vote, I recommend the book *Mothers of Feminism* by Margaret Hope Bacon). People of faith, new wine, new prophets were emerging—black, white, male, and female. Finally, slaves were emancipated and women got the right to vote, though full equality was far from complete. Poverty, segregation, and many horrors awaited the freed slaves. Overall, the freed slaves did not get their promised forty acres and a mule.

With World War II behind us, it appeared that good times were here. But it was good times only for part of the country. The nasty cancers of poverty, racism, and inequality were still present. Then, from a church in Alabama, a new young leader emerged, the Rev. Dr. Martin Luther King, Jr. King found himself drawn and called out of the local church to lead a national movement for equality and justice emerging out of his Christian faith and the biblical witness—powerful new wine emerging from the old winery of biblical faith. Numerous black and white voices of faith joined in, as well as people of other faiths and colors, as well as people of no faith.

In the 1960s in Latin America, out of the teeming masses of the poor and oppressed, there emerged what has been called Liberation theologies. All of these voices in both the U.S. and Latin America cried out that God loves and has a deep concern for the poor of the earth, that they should be treated fairly and justly. The second half of the twentieth century was a tumultuous time in both North and South America, as well as all around Africa, rising out of the injustices of colonialism. For many, the connection of assisting the oppressed was obvious, drawing great hope and inspiration from the pivotal story of the Exodus, as well as by the Prophets and Jesus. Thus, the largest new wine of the last fifty years or more, and as strong as ever now, is the call to do the work of justice and reconciliation, bringing together all God's children.

I know there are some, or many, of the faithful who might say that they affirm the biblical prophetic call, but add that not all people are called to be prophets. While that is true, nevertheless, every church should have a prophetic voice. People must hear messages about this wider call in worship and study these topics. Then the church can encourage those in their congregation who are feeling this call to action.

Reflection Questions

1. Share what your awareness is about the various social and faith movements discussed in this chapter.

2. What is your understanding of how God works in modern history?

Chapter 7. Discipleship and the Way of Jesus

Although it is not comical, I do find the following a bit amusing. The presence of so many incidents of conflict between Jesus and the religious leaders have led some scholars to say roughly, "Let's take it a little easier on these Pharisees, Sadducees and lawyers—most were probably respectable, nice guys who performed their religious functions as prescribed. Cut them some slack, they were just doing their jobs." The problem with that is that almost all religious or political leaders can and do say, "I am just doing my job," along with a boatload of more justifications that simply won't do. The Prophets and Jesus believed that the work of the religious leaders is of great importance—it is God's work! They exclaimed that to do their work wrongly, and ultimately harmfully, is not acceptable. With leadership and power comes great responsibility. Therefore, the prophets and Jesus lash out at leaders when they go off track, for when they go off track, the people usually follow.

I add Paul into this discussion with a few of his statements. He writes: "For the whole law is summed up in a single commandment, 'You shall love your neighbor as yourself.'" (Galations 5:14 and also Romans 8) In fact, Paul goes to great length and passion in Galatians and elsewhere stressing the theme that we are set free from the Law, declaring, "For freedom Christ has set us free. Stand firm, therefore, and do not submit again to a yoke of slavery" [to the Law]. (Gal 5:1) Again from Paul, "Christ has abolished the law with its commandments and ordinances, that he might create in himself one new humanity in place of the two, thus making peace, and might reconcile both groups (Jews and Gentiles) to God in one body through the cross, thus putting to death that hostility through it." (Ephesians 2:15-16)

Liberating news! The mass of religious laws are replaced by the commandment to love!

Does that mean that the Jesus Way is simple and easy? Certainly not. To love all God's children, to love even those who are different, to love our enemies—is hard. And so Jesus explicitly told us that His way is narrow and hard, but it leads to life. Simple in concept, often hard in practice—paradox again.

When I look at Christianity in the world, it appears that the majority of the more than two billion Christians (including all those with any form of affiliation with one of the denominations) choose one of two paths—and both present problems. This returns to a theme I discuss in another place as well.

I exaggerate a little, but one option is the fundamentalist reduction, which practices an easy path—just say the words "Jesus is my Lord" and you are set. There is an incomplete truth in that important assertion, because Jesus makes clear that saying his name without doing his word does not cut it—and he states it more strongly than that. Yes, these adherents do some good works, which is wonderful, but they often do not address the deep problems confronting God's children. They almost live as if all is well. Yet all is not well in the world—God's world. Therefore we cannot ignore deep and difficult realities by evading the full call of discipleship. It is not as easy as they present—it is hard—as Jesus indicates.

Any discussion of the church in the world must include the Roman Catholic church because of its sheer size, power, and wealth. In many ways it is almost "too big to discuss," and yet I want to present a problem that I see. In short, the Catholic church has re-created an enormous and elaborate religious system of practices, doctrines, obligations, and laws. They have some brilliant minds, superb canon lawyers, who can argue and defend them impressively. I sometimes have been swayed by their explanations. The intent of this vast system is surely good, and the large system of Catholic education helps explain and instill this large corpus of obligations and practices to live by. Make it a habit early, and it becomes rote, automatic, ingrained. The danger is that it becomes a return to the Law, in contrast to Jesus and Paul, who said that we are freed from the religious Law, and that it is all summed up in the Great Commandments to "Love God, and love your neighbor." It appears that the Roman Catholic leadership feels that the people can't handle the truth that sets you free when they basically teach "just follow our system." However, because of the explosion of higher education, the opening up of the Bible, along with the pedophilia and cover-up scandal, that old wine is not working for more and more Catholics—at least in the western world.

Yet within Catholicism there have been fascinating alternative voices and movements. In the second half of the 20th century in Latin America, which was overwhelmingly Catholic, an important movement emerged. Before that, the church was often aligned with the ruling powers—usually dictators—telling the huge majority of poor people to accept their lot in life. Liberation theology emerged and spread rapidly, offering a different message. Some priests and Catholic thinkers argued persuasively and biblically that God aligns with the poor and oppressed, just as God did in the Exodus! God does not wish for people to suffer in poverty. Archbishop Oscar Romero was martyred while saying mass for speaking out in El Salvador. Pope Francis has made Romero a saint. Parallel to Martin Luther King Jr. in the US, parts of the church in Latin America walked with the poor masses. It got messy and bloody. After a few years, John Paul II was elected as pope. He used his great influence to help overthrow communism in his homeland Poland. But then (some say it was due to the influence of Cardinal Ratzinger), John Paul II rejected

Liberation theology. It's puzzling that he helped push political change in his homeland but said no to the movement of liberation all over Central and South America. Cardinal Ratzinger followed John Paul II as Pope Benedict.

I argue that, at this time, all the churches, including the Roman Catholic Church, need to move out of their old wineskins and be transformed. Pope Francis has offered, and continues to offer, bold, direct, hopeful, and challenging statements that equate to new wine for this time—like Jesus did in adapting the original teachings to the needs and problems of his time. He is an advocate for the poor, and he cares about social justice. It would be wonderful to have many more people from both the Catholic and fundamentalist folds joining in these holy tasks of working with and assisting those whom Jesus called "the least of these, my brothers and sisters" (Matthew 25:31ff). It remains to be seen how much Pope Francis can change this enormous hierarchical institution. And what happens after Francis (he is in his 80s)?

What Jesus presented forcefully is a Way of life that encompasses all of life. And as Quaker William Penn said, "God does not call us out of the world, but sends us into it, to mend the world."

A great challenge I observe is that although many religious folk would say God comes first, in reality and practice, I observe that too many people, religious and non-religious, put nation or tribe first. That makes it much easier to demonize and attack other nations and peoples. The track record of excessive nationalism has left a very bloody trail in history. We note that Jesus reached out to people beyond his own "tribe." He had interactions with various categories of outsiders, including several Samaritans, the Roman centurion, the Canaanite woman, and women in general (who were relegated to second class status at best). He praises the faith of the centurion, exclaiming, "not even in all Israel have I seen such faith" (Luke 7:9), and again in Matthew 8:10. He points affirmatively to the persistence of the Canaanite woman, and he treats the Samaritan woman at the well as fully one of God's children. Jesus' actions speak as loud as his words and demonstrate God's care and love for both Jews and Gentiles—for all the world. He is living out the Abrahamic promise that the people of Abraham would be a light to the nations. Both Paul and Peter learned that the gospel and the love of God are offered to all people. So also are we called to engage and care for all people, looking for ways to reconcile, to break down hostilities and inequalities, while maintaining or building both beloved faith communities and wider communities of acceptance, understanding, and equality. Paul teaches us that we are God's "ambassadors of reconciliation" (II Corinthians 5:19ff).

The widely known parable of the Good Samaritan has lost its original shock value. Everyone gets the message to help out the person in need. Some are not startled that the two religious leaders walked past the bleeding person in need, failing to love their neighbor, and even more striking that the one who does show compassion was from a disdained tribe of people—the Samaritans. The hearers of Jesus' time would have heard this story with some wide-eyed astonishment, and some were likely offended. Without compassion, mercy, justice, and love, religion is bankrupt, according to Jesus. "As you did it not to the least of these brothers and sisters, you did it not to me" (Matt 25:31ff). And in that parable, those who were not compassionate were turned away from the heavenly kingdom. Thus, the one following in the Way of Jesus, whether knowingly or unknowingly, fulfills the commandment to love thy neighbor, thereby fulfills the Law—and Jesus invites them into his kingdom. Thankfully, in these times, there are a growing number of people of faith who understand this wonderful revelation in the parable. If we deeply reflect on Jesus' Way, we see that people in other traditions, or no tradition, can follow along Jesus' Way. Jesus said so, declaring several times that it is those who do what he teaches that are faithful and true followers. And most dramatically, in the parable of the last judgment in Matthew 25 he powerfully indicates that it is those who lived in this Way, to whom it is said "inherit the kingdom prepared for you from the foundation of the world; for I was hungry and you gave me food; for I was thirsty and you gave me drink; I was a stranger and you welcomed me; I was sick and you visited me; I was in prison and you came to me." Then those righteous will ask (my paraphrase), and "when did we see you so as to do that?" 'And the King will answer, 'Truly I say to you, as you did it to one of the least of these my brothers and sisters, you did it to me.'" That's quite clear. And it demonstrates that God measures us by love, especially towards those in deepest need, yet love over all. God thus invites such people into his kingdom. Beautiful. The notion that the humble, compassionate, broken person who does not know God, but who does what she or he can to assist and care for others—does the loving thing, a person such as Gandhi who gives most of his us adult life to help the people of India and was assassinated—that such people are doomed to torment and hell by a God of love just because they fail a creedal test. What kind of God would that be? Yet, this is sometimes believed and has been said (I have heard it), and based on that I can empathize with those who say that they reject such a religion. The Bible states that God is love. God can be angry at human evil, but ultimately God strives like the prodigal son's father to bring back all his wayward children.

Does this, and even the title of my book, point us to a world without religion, without churches and synagogues, and numerous religious days and practices? My best answer is Yes and No. I have talked about Jesus blasting through, knocking down, or altering so much of religion. Therefore, I answer "Yes" in that way. Yet there is a No. We must have beloved communities. We cannot effectively be disciples without deep, dedicated, committed communities of caring and action. This vital necessity means we need something like the church and synagogue, yet re-emerging in new wineskins. The biblical Greek word for church means *those called out*. That does not automatically imply a vast and intricate entity with hundreds of laws, practices and obligations. We must be vigilant about not letting a great conglomeration of religious practices, ritual, and pageantry overrun, hide, or demote the simple, yet challenging Way of life that Jesus taught. He said it very directly and repeatedly in his stern responses to religious leaders, challenging them, "Woe, to you scribes and Pharisees, hypocrites! For you tithe mint, dill and cumin, and have neglected the weightier matters of the law: justice and mercy and faith. . . You blind guides! You strain out a gnat but swallow a camel!" (Matthew 23:23) Wouldn't it have been something to hear Jesus speak?

There is an additional component of religion, or if one prefers, spiritual practice that is needed. It is the inner journey, meaning a practice of centering prayer and meditation. Both religious and many nonreligious use some form of these practices. The religious person connects through these to God. Though I won't discuss the inner journey in detail, it is crucial and necessary. The inner life lets the roots of our core beliefs grow deep and become a part of who we are. It helps to form our beliefs, desires, and goals— thus our life. If the roots are not deep, they can be uprooted and blown away. Like the training and practice of a musician or athlete, it is critical. The inner journey must remain the vehicle and practice by which we commune with God, opening up to the transforming message and reality of God's love.

I find myself working and praying for the success of this new awakening or re-emergence or transformation of religion and the church. Some of the present structures, organizations, corruption, and cultural distortions need to fall or break down. That can be upsetting or frightening. It is like finding cancer in various parts of a body requiring serious surgery, as well as other treatments. As we know from medicine, sometimes surgery must be done. There are many denominations, so there are many surgeries to be done, but we can take inspiration from the knowledge that quite a few successful surgeries have already occurred or are underway. Let me leave that analogy, for analogies have their limitations. However, I believe we need more of the breakdown of the old forms and abuses of the past, so we can move forward with the hard work of new wineskins. With humility, boldness, imagination, study, and prayer we must continue creating new ministries. The new communities should exude vitality and fullness of life, causing people to notice and be drawn, even as the early churches did, as they became known as a people of a remarkable Way.

To the seemingly growing number of people leaving religion, this book is an urgent response that says, "I agree with you in terms of throwing out the dirty bath water (of religion), but I want to tell you why you should not throw out the baby." If we constantly work on throwing out the dirty water, we find the baby, emerging as Jesus, bringing us the truly fulfilling Way of Life, which is the Way of Love. As simple and trite as this sounds, my experience tells me that people know that Love is what matters. More people will be attracted to a community where love is obvious, and who go out into the world boldly loving their neighbor. This practice, as John wrote, will lead people to exclaim "See those Christians how they love one another."

If we follow through deeply with the spirit of Jesus' teachings, we must continually watch for, over centuries and millennia, the incessant growth of weeds, just as we do with gardens! The religious weeds can hide the transforming Jesus or present deceptive distortions. We lose sight of and forget that Jesus continually talked about how we live our earthly lives and how we treat each other. By ignoring that truth, we make him a Jesus without Jesus—we make him a theological doctrine and mechanism to get to heaven without the earthly Jesus who walked among the people, teaching, forgiving, and bringing God's kingdom near. When we take seriously what Jesus said and did, it leads to major changes in the way that we follow him. "Go into the world . . . teaching them to obey everything I have commanded you" (Matthew 28: 20). Following Jesus is more something that you do than it is an assent to doctrine or recitation of a creed. It is he who said so, proclaiming that some will come to him in the Judgment saying "Did we not do many things in your name," and to whom he responds, "Depart from me you evildoers."(Matthew 7:22-23).

The faithful life that follows Jesus leads to liberation—"If you continue in my word, you are truly my disciples, and you will know the truth, and the truth will make you free." (John 8;31-32) This gift of freedom frees us to bear more magnificent fruit. Simply put, remembering to put the whole Jesus into Jesus radically alters the life of discipleship. It cannot remain simply "Thank you Jesus for my ticket to heaven, see you then!" Instead, it becomes more of a "thank you Jesus for the message of God's love and forgiveness (salvation). And please empower us to serve you with courage by proclaiming the Good News, loving God and loving our neighbors as ourselves—as you so powerfully taught us. May we be bold, compassionate and just."

I heard a South American faith leader, Juan Carlos Ortiz, explain the difference between Christianity as doctrine and Christianity as a Way, a Way of love. In a very clear and engaging manner, he criticized messages or ministers that focus heavily on all the history and scholarship surrounding scripture, for making sermons closer to a lecture, with a pretty ending in which you are told to go out and do good. He compared it to the example of a mother who wants her young child to take a bath and clean up. Ortiz asks: Does the mother say, "I would like you to take a bath now. You will use soap in your bath. Soap is made of the following ingredients, coming from all over the world. It contains several ingredients produced in India, still others from Argentina, and several chemicals manufactured in Germany. Next I will explain to you how each ingredient works in the process of cleaning you up, so you understand how it kills germs and makes you clean. Then you will rinse off, and then dry off with this towel. This towel is made from fibers produced in a factory not far from here, and as it rubs along your skin it absorbs the moisture and removes lingering dirt. So please go and do this." With a raised, energetic voice, Ortiz continues, "No! My mother said, "go take a bath right now and get clean." And with a little help from a hand on my back, she exclaimed "Get in that tub and clean yourself up. Now!" It made me chuckle, and it had the feel of the direct and pointed teachings of Jesus. Let Ortiz's story be a parable, urging you not to be so caught up in information that you miss the transforming power in Jesus' message. Let his story both amuse and shake you from the temptation of on-the-couch or in-the-pew Christianity to one of loving engagement and bold action out in the world. Ortiz is right when he adds, "Jesus did not come primarily to inform life—he came to form life." Discipleship formation is life transformation. Paul declared, "If a person is in Christ, s(he) is a new creation. The old is finished and gone, behold the new is come." (2 Corinthians 5: 17ff) Yes, go ahead and do some study, but ultimately get up and get out there and live it. Do the loving and right and just thing—now!

Reflection Questions

1. Jesus and the prophets called justice one of the "weightier matters" of the Law and of following him. The work of justice and reconciliation can push one into the public and political sphere. It is messy, often hard, and complicated. If many of God's people (and God desires everyone to be in relationship with him) are suffering or mistreated or denied justice and equality, how can it be okay for large numbers of Christians to not get more involved in the public sphere by saying "it's not my thing?" Discuss.

Chapter 8. The God of Jesus

According as (people's) notions of God are, such will their reli-gion be; if they have gross and false conceptions of God, their religion will be absurd and superstitious. If they fancy God to be an ill-natured Being, armed with infinite power, who takes delight in the misery and ruin of his creatures, and is ready to take all advantages against them, they may fear him, but they will hate him; and they will be apt to be such towards one another, as they fancy God to be towards them; for all religion doth naturally incline men to imitate him whom they worship. [7]

This statement by English Archbishop Matthew Tindall two centuries ago captures the great importance of how we understand and conceive of God, and in particular, the destructive effect of a fearsome, harsh, and violent conception.

Thank God, Jesus offers a different perspective on God. That is the purpose of this chapter.

After hitting rock bottom, the Prodigal son in Jesus' parable prepared his confession and plea that he would make to his father (representing God) when he returned home. The prodigal says, "I will get up, and go to my father, and I will say to him, 'Father, I have sinned against heaven and before you. I am no longer worthy to be called your son; treat me like one of your hired hands'. So he set off and went to his father. But while he was still far off, his father saw him and was filled with compassion; he ran and put his arms around him and kissed him. . .the father said to his servants, 'Quickly, bring out the best robe and put it on him; put a ring on his hand, and shoes on his feet. Let us celebrate. And bring the fatted calf and kill it. And let us eat and make merry; for this my son was dead and is alive again; he was lost and is found.'"

---

7   Hawk, L. Daniel. *The Violence of the Biblical God Canonical Narrative and Christian Faith*, 2019, p. 5.

(Luke 15:18-24)

What a dramatically different portrayal of God from the many righteously angry, punitive, and violent images of God in the Old Testament! We need to carefully reflect and pray on how we conceive of God, or else our efforts to build new, healthy, faithful beloved communities will not be healthy. The key in making this journey is to look afresh to Jesus as the person and principle to shape our understanding of God. Jesus demonstrates this reshaped image of God by both his teaching and his life. The God that Jesus reveals to us is a compelling and striking metamorphosis from a frequently angry, violent, warrior king God to a loving God seeking and saving his lost children. The repercussions of this change are huge.

To see this major transformation requires that we tackle a harsh, ugly challenge. Although the old Testament contains majestic and wonderful passages and images of God as one who wants to provide for, care, and guide His difficult, wayward children, yet we also find quite a number of passages portraying a God as One who is very jealous, flying into rages and meting out brutal and even lethal punishment. These actions include the killing not only of pagan peoples, but also sometimes of the Hebrew people, whom He has chosen. When the Hebrews moved into Canaan, God instructed them in the book of Joshua to wage holy war—jihad—commanding them to "kill everything that lives and moves and has breath" of the peoples and animals that they conquer. Later God defeated the Egyptians, and slaughtered many of their children. The prophets speak of God trying to call His people back from their sins, but ultimately brutally punishing the sinful Jewish kingdoms of both the south and north, the Babylonians crushing one and the Assyrians the other. In an age of brutal conquest, historians note that the Assyrians were particularly cruel to the peoples they conquered—merciless. Even with the presence of moments of mercy at other times, we cannot sidestep those actions and those portrayals of a volatile and brutal God.

Although some might think the following biblical passage entertaining (which I used to think), is it really? There is an episode in Genesis involving Abraham where he tries to cool down God's wrath by bargaining with Him. God's wrath was ignited by the sinful city of Sodom. Abraham asked God to spare Sodom, and like a skillful lawyer he makes his case. He opens by asking that if 50 righteous people could be found, would He spare the town? Once agreed, he proposed 40, and God acquiesced. Abraham continued on down to just 10 righteous people, with God conceding to each reduction. Abraham was able to change God's plan, unfortunately, even ten could not be found, so God executed his burning anger, literally.

The scriptures also include statements such as, "and God repented of the evil he was about to do" (Exodus 32:14), along with multiple occasions when God changed His mind. That phrase causes me trouble. If God is all that we say God is, then why would God be changing His mind? Biblical lawyers and scholars undoubtedly have tried to work their magic around these difficulties, but it is ultimately bluster and double-talk wrapped in scholarship and erudition. Such exercises of intellect are not synonymous with truth. Of course, neither are they antonyms. The gospels indicate that Jesus interacted and disputed with religious leaders and lawyers almost as if their roles were interchangeable. More of the troubling portrayals of God in the Older Testament could be added, but I think it is clear enough that there is a problem here. We are given a deeply anthropomorphic picture of God, which consequently renders God not only loving and kind but also volatile, violent, and jealous.

Some argue that the true God has a right to be jealous. Isn't that odd? If one of my children or grandchildren said they loved another out-of-family adult more than me, I suppose I would be upset or jealous or both, but I would not brutalize or kill them. And God is surely better than us, not more dangerous. Let's see if there is a way out of this.

Given the world of kings, warriors, conflict and conquest, that has dominated history in those times (and all through history), the early biblical writers tried to convey the superiority and greatness of God. With what they observed, they could only conceive of God as a male, king, and warrior, full of human emotions and volatility. So this portrayal of God in the Bible still dwells deep in the human psyche—casting a shadow over the loving images also found in scripture. As a result people often believe, or feel on a subconscious level, that it is necessary to resort to punitive and violent measures with enemies and evildoers, swiftly resorting to war, retribution, and punishment. For a longer, scholarly dive into this biblical challenge, I would point you to a book by a Christian old testament scholar named L. Daniel Hawk. The book is titled *The Violence of the Biblical God: canonical narrative and Christian faith*" (see footnote 9).

This perspective influences even parenting practices, reflecting the biblical saying "spare the rod and spoil the child" (Proverbs 13:24), and the Mosaic teaching of stoning a rebellious son (Deuteronomy 21:18f), and more. Such teachings help to create a belief in an inevitable cycle of violence, which can be biblically supported. In this view, war and punishment are a significant part of God's plan and operation. Looking around the world now, we continue to hear some religious voices operating from a warrior God perspective. However, Jesus transforms this as we will see later.

Generally speaking, this violence and punishment mindset is much stronger and deeper for males than females (not saying that women are without sin). History, crime statistics, and daily life overwhelmingly demonstrate this. History as recorded until very recently is filled with the story of mostly men going to war and conquest for countless reasons. It is rare to find a man who, if provoked enough, will not resort to violence (Christian men included), especially if the other person is *different*—in skin color, religion, nationality, political viewpoint.

Because this warrior image and mentality is so deep-seated, it is not enough to only say that God wishes otherwise, like a raging father who hugs his children one day and beats them the next day saying "this hurts me more than it hurts you." God is surely better than that, not worse. Some religious leaders still reinforce this; consequently, numerous followers readily believe that endless punishment and torture await the multitudes of sinners and unbelievers. And because human disobedience continues, the story of this world is a large cycle of violence and punishment for all but the chosen. Sadly, this has appealed to many male religious leaders as well as to male political leaders, who gain power and influence through fear and readily support the case for war and punishment.

When God is seen as a male, it easily leads to the subjugation, and even abuse, of women. In addition to the development of divine right monarchy, the father was quickly established as the divinely authorized head of the house. Add to that the punishment and revenge narrative and we see the difficult task ahead of rethinking what God is like, as well as what it means to be a man. I offer here a short personal discussion of this. I grew up in the center of Brooklyn (only two blocks from the intersection of Flatbush and Church avenues). Legend holds that Brooklyn is a place of danger, fighting, and crime. Not surprising in a place of nearly three million people, but in my experience it wasn't too bad (overall I loved growing up in Brooklyn). To qualify that, on a day-to-day street level as a young male there were so many things that could trigger confrontation—it could be a perceived *dis* (disrespect) in sports, a certain gesture, talking to somebody's girl, ranking each other out, on up to more serious encounters, when a "true man" must defend his manhood, often physically. There is nothing more challenging than to be told, "Be a man! Man up! Are you gonna take that? Don't be a _____." You had to save face at all costs, according to the unwritten code of manhood or machismo. That is not just a Brooklyn problem. Is there any place on the planet where machismo is not a large reality? This discussion has a two-fold connection to the concept of honor. To honor God is right. To honor another person as equal and possessing dignity is good and noble. To dishonor is therefore wrong. When honor and dishonor mix with the warrior narrative, too often the outcome descends into violence and destruction. It brings to mind the example of Alexander Hamilton (now writ large with the impressive Broadway show bearing his name), a brilliant young founder of this country, who lost his life in a gun duel over the perception of having been dishonored. So goes a never-ending stream of violence from bloody noses to shootings and even large-scale slaughter and war.

I particularly loved playing sports, especially basketball, playing in school yards all around Brooklyn. You needed to learn to put on your "game face" and crush your opponent. That meant you were often only one step away from physical confrontation. Sports have often been considered as good preparation for the military, for you always sacrifice for the team ("there is no I in team"), you take the pain, you do not surrender, you play to win at all costs. With near universality, people throughout history have seen the ultimate man or hero as a warrior.

Raising this discussion does not mean I do not appreciate the sacrifice of millions of men (and now women) who have been wounded or died for their country. But it is quite tragic that the predominant narrative of history remains constant conflict and war—meaning that millions of young men and women must keep on dying in this way. So I agree that we must thank and honor those who serve, are wounded, or die in defense of country, and yet can we forget how bloody tragic this is? Is war required so that we can make heroes? Is war and violence the inevitable nature of life and of history? We need some help from strong, compassionate women and God.

This seeming digression into the male propensity for violence is widely illustrated in the Old Testament. This violent image of masculinity was seen as a normal part of being male in biblical days, so that the best image that the ancient Hebrews (and most other cultures as well) could conjure up for God was of a mighty warrior King—and it still prevails for many. I can hear a cacophony of voices objecting: "God always wants to love and bring back his rebellious, sinful people!" Yes, but because they continue to be disobedient, God must ultimately pulverize them in countless ways. In the psyche of many, if you're bad, maybe we give you a few second chances. But then punishment, even savage, endless punishment is required from human hands and from the "God of love." In the realm of crime and punishment it is considered executing justice, which is vastly different from the prophetic call to do justice. We frequently see, at the outcome of a criminal trial, the aggrieved crying out *we want justice!*, or *justice was not done!*" Crime and punishment, war and victory, are overwhelming narratives of history. It is bloody and tragic.

Another Way

Is there another way? Theologian John Cobb's recent book, *Jesus' Abba*[8], argues that since God is Love, God does not operate by military force and violence. Jesus rejected violence and revenge. Because God operates by love, which is God's essence, we observe in life and in history that sometimes *in the short run*, God's efforts do not always succeed. War and violence carry the day. God

8   Cobb, John B. 2016. *Jesus' Abba: the God Who Has Not Failed.* [Neither publisher nor place of publication identified]: https://muse.jhu.edu/book/45424/.

always desires love—it is human beings who choose violence and war. This distinction is crucial—and we no longer have to say that the tragedy and bloodshed of history has been part of God's plan. We can reject that. Human beings have freedom, and they often choose the road of violence. Followers of Jesus can say that such things are not God's plan. Isn't that good news?

Should we not be glad that God is not a warrior at heart? And yet, some readers told Cobb, "Your God is a wimp." Revealing! Indeed, Jesus offered no fight, no resistance to his arrest and crucifixion. Does that make Jesus a wimp? I maintain that the non-violent power and example of Jesus is courageous and strong. The determination, perseverance, and strength demonstrated in facing violence and death until his last earthly breath was truly courageous and powerful. And witness the result of Jesus' short life and death by Roman crucifixion—something incredibly powerful obviously happened, something history-making and epic.

Fork in the Road

On a beautiful Spring day I was walking in the main quadrangle of Brooklyn College (part of the City University of New York). A young man was standing behind a table holding a large book in his hand, which turned out to be the Hebrew scriptures. I approached him, and we engaged in friendly conversation. At some point the question of Jesus as the Messiah came up, and I said Jesus was God's Messiah, God's Anointed One. He calmly disagreed. And he explained that it clearly says in the Hebrew Scriptures that the Messiah would be a king like David. Jesus did not become a king like David and did not restore Israel to glory. Therefore, he concluded, Jesus could not be the Messiah.

I come now to an important fork in the road regarding Jesus. I will take one of the choices. In doing so I want to make very clear that, while I differ with the other choice, I wish no ill or violence or destruction for those who have made the other choice. To wish violence on others is to contradict Jesus. Having said that, I proceed.

Though the gospels say that Jesus is "of the house and lineage of David," Jesus did not pursue the kingship of Israel, at least in the earthly sense. When King Herod interrogated him, Jesus made no reply. Just as Jesus turned over various religious traditions with declarations saying "You have heard that it was said. . . but I say unto you" Jesus boldly moved beyond or superseded some Jewish teachings. Similarly, Jesus stated that his kingdom is "not of this world." His teachings point to beloved communities that will cause people to say, "See those Christians, how they love one another." And he taught, "This commandment I give you, that you love one another as I have loved you." (John15:12)Thus, Jesus came as a different sort of king, disappointing those who wanted to see a new and mighty political king. Some will say that at the end of times, we will see Jesus as such a king, and we are told that in the end God will make all things new—I will leave it at that for now. That Jesus showed us a different kind of kingship returns us to the prevailing understandings of God in his time—that of a mighty warrior, desiring to love his children, yet because of their continual failings, must punish and destroy. Twenty centuries later, these images of God remain strong, for they are in the Bible, and they resonate with history.

A number of Christian thinkers assert that Jesus' use of *Abba* to address God is very important. He used it as the opening of the Lord's Prayer—*Abba, who art in heaven*, and he used it in the garden of Gethsemane on the night before he was crucified (Mark 14:36 and also in Luke 11)—two key moments. Paul also used *Abba* on several occasions, particularly the passage where he tells us that we are all adopted children of God ("When we cry *Abba*, it is that very Spirit bearing witness with our spirit that we are all children of God." Romans 8:15). *Abba* is the Aramaic for father, indicating a deep intimacy and respect between father and often a child. That is a cosmic leap from God as the Holy Other, or the frightening king you dare not come near to—jumping all the way to the loving father/parent in the parable of the Prodigal Son. John Cobb writes: "But there is another theme that runs through the Bible as a whole, but is especially accented by Jesus. God is neither cosmic ruler nor moral judge. God is love. And Jesus proposes that the image of that love is the love of an infant's father, that is, "Abba." Control and judgment fade into the background; tenderness and unconditional acceptance are central."[9] He adds: "The more we reflect on Jesus' understanding of his Abba, the more it can seem to us that he should have spoken of God, not as his father but as his mother."[10]

This may rattle some people. I propose saying that God displays a very compelling combination of stereotypically feminine attributes along with some that are stereotypically masculine. Shouldn't we be at a point to realize that tenderness, abundant forgiveness, compassion, mercy, etc. can and should be masculine traits as well? I argue that this leads to a truer and fuller understanding of God, as well as a better definition of manhood. The key point is that we are offered an altered portrayal of the nature of God.

The scholar Moltmann adds to this discussion: "The special characteristic of Jesus' relationship to God is made clear in the *Abba* prayer (the Lord's Prayer). In order to correct later misrepresentations, it is important to come back again and again to the intimacy of this prayer of Jesus. In Aramaic, *Abba* is baby language. It is the word children use for their original person of reference. Whether it be mother or father."[11] He goes on to say, "Jesus demonstrates this

---

9   *Ibid*, p. 122.
10   *Ibid*, pp. 13-14.
11   Moltmann, Jürgen. *The Way of Jesus Christ*. S.C.M. Press., 1990, p. 142.

nearness of God by 'having mercy' and 'compassion' on the poor and suffering; and by doing so he substantiates God's 'feminine' attributes (Isaiah 49:15; 66:13)." [12]

When Jesus instructed, "Go and learn what this means, "I (God) desire mercy and not sacrifice" (Hosea 6:6), he did more than just reprimand a Pharisee. Jesus was building on the prophetic insight that pointed towards mercy and compassion as not only higher than religious practice, but the actual fulfillment of religion, transmuting it into a Way of living—which is, ultimately, love in action. The prophets introduced new wine, and Jesus was introducing more.

Even as I have embraced the simple, stunning words of John (see I John 4:7ff) telling us that "Everyone who loves knows God, for God is love" (repeated again later in the passage), I still have hard moments wondering if God is yet the strict God of punishment. How many millions of people through the past and until this day have cringed and feared at what they believe is a stern father God? Think about the title of a famed sermon, "*Sinners in the Hands of an Angry God,*" by Jonathan Edwards in the 18th century, what a horrible predicament, for we are all sinners and God is angry—angry with hell fire waiting for a large portion of humanity. No doubt that is the appeal of a Christianity reduced to a few words, such that if you recite the right words, you're safe. I imagine there is an outcry from some Christians. "Isn't that exactly right?" For decades I have pondered this question, and I find I must answer, yes and no. Yes, if that declaration of words includes a true change of heart, a change of life, a reorientation of how you live life, what is called *repentance*. No, if it is a lifeless statement of information like "water is made up of two hydrogen atoms and one oxygen atom," as if that statement is merely words, sound vibrations in air. Christianity is not passing a theology exam. Rather it is a Way of living, that is launched by a change of heart.

12   *Ibid*, p. 142.

How can I dare to say these things? Let's check with Jesus. In the parable of the Last Judgment (in Matthew 25:31ff), he said we will be judged on how much we have cared for others, particularly "the least of these, my brothers and sisters." He did not say, "But if you just say certain words, you slip in through another door." Jesus' way is the way of Love, not the way of doctrinal assent. Jesus was repeatedly tough on those who simply hear, but do not DO his word. Recently I enjoyed listening to a preacher say—"There will not be a test at the end, such as, answer this: Virgin Birth, a) Disagree strongly; b) Disagree; c) Agree; d) Agree Strongly." And so on.

A significant number of people (a majority in the past?) had their fearful view of God reinforced by a father who was intimidating, the enforcer, and sometimes more than that, dangerously violent. That could easily make their sense and understanding of God even less comforting. What about the biblical admonition, "the fear of the Lord is the beginning of wisdom." I think a better translation is to use the word awe. We should be in awe of the Creator of this universe. Beyond that, I have chosen to turn to John in the New Testament, "there is no fear in love, for perfect love casts out fear" (I John 4:7ff). The following example is instructive.

In the late 20th century a program called Scared Straight was sending former prisoners around the country. The idea was to have these tough guys tell young people about the horrors of prison to scare them straight, in the sense of avoiding crime. To "scare the living hell out of them" with the threat of eternal torment and hell was (and still is) an old and core technique of religion. It is not just those who reject or are unaware of much of modern science that believe in a hell of torment and torture. This part of Christian teaching has come under increasing scrutiny, raising questions as to whether there is a hell, or what that could mean. From totalitarian regimes, to religious extremists, to a significant portion of religion, to crime syndicates and gangs, have shown that fear, threat, and violence can be very effective for changing behavior—though rarely a change of heart, as in repentance. As the Bishop said in the opening quote of this chapter, a threatening image of God does not yield loving and devoted followers.

Leaping forward to the late 20th century, in her novel *Paradise,* Toni Morrison captured the clash of competing perceptions of God. Through the character of Lone Dupres she describes a woman who was able to detect above the troubled and violent environment of her town, and the oppressive, intimidating declarations of the ministers, she found a God who is liberating—a God who guides and teaches and points us into His world.

The gospels show us Jesus coming from God, speaking of God, and pointing to how we should live in God's world. Following Jesus is about trying to do God's will. Thus, it is more than simply thanking Jesus for what he has done without diving deeply into building the Kingdom-Community of God—a central focus of his proclamation. Praising Jesus without truly following him I call "Jesus without Jesus."

Reflection Questions

1. Reflect on and discuss your image of God.

2. How do you address the deeply disturbing actions attributed to God in various parts of the Bible?

3. Discuss the approach of using Jesus as the lens to understand God and the Bible.

4. Discuss the phrase "Jesus without Jesus," as presented in this book.

Chapter 9. More on Jesus' New Wine of Revelation

I do not believe that one has to study cosmology to see that the ancient, pre-scientific world view with heaven up there and hell down below (inside the earth?) is not accurate. The gospel of John says, "God is Spirit." Ultimately, God is more than we can conceive. We would be lost, but for the fact that we believe that God "was in Christ, reconciling the world to Himself" (II Corinthians 5:17ff). We get a glimpse into the "heart" of God by what we see in the life and teachings of Jesus. That is where I center this book. We observe that there are numerous encounters where Jesus heals and forgives men and women, Israelites and foreigners, the marginalized and outcasts, loving and inviting all. Add to that the beautiful list where Paul writes that the "fruit of the Spirit (thus God) is love, joy, peace, patience, kindness, generosity, faithfulness, gentleness, self-control" (Gal. 5:22-23). Therefore God has the best attributes conceivable for both men and women, and it is long overdue to explicitly declare attributes in God that we normally call feminine. Others have been making this case for decades, trying to lead us out of the pathological aspects of patriarchy. Recall the moment where Jesus is approaching Jerusalem and sighs, "O Jerusalem, Jerusalem, who kills the prophets and stones to death those who have been sent to her! How often I wanted to gather your children together as a hen gathers her chicks under her wings, but you were unwilling!" (Matthew 23:37). I also assert that we must always realize that our descriptions of God will be incomplete, because God is surely beyond and greater than what we can conceive. But thank Jesus, we have received wonderful news and glimpses of God and God's purposes.

Continuing with the changes, even contrast, between Jesus' revelation and the ways of history, consider the episode where

Jesus hears the disciples arguing over who is the greatest in the kingdom, and who will sit at Jesus' right and left. And Jesus said to them: "You know that among the Gentiles those whom they recognize as their rulers lord it over them, and their great ones are tyrants over them. But it shall not be so among you; but whoever would be great among you must be your servant, and whoever would be first among you must be slave of all. For the Son of Man came not to be served but to serve, and to give his life a ransom for many" (Mark 10: 42-45).That is quite a change from traditional views of greatness.

Jesus also said: "You have heard that it was said, 'you shall love your neighbor and hate your enemy.' But I say to you, love your enemies and pray for those who persecute you, so that you may be children of your Father in heaven; for he makes his sun rise on the evil and on the good, and sends rain on the righteous and on the unrighteous." (Matt 5: 43-45).

These transformational teachings serve to counteract the prevalence of hating and destroying your enemy in all times, moving people towards the goal of mercy. It points out another difference between the kingdom of God and the kingdoms of this world. In modern times we rarely speak of kingdoms, instead we have nations or nation-states, somewhere near 200 of them. When we see the Olympics, this world of nations seems like quite a wonderful thing. However nationalism, so prevalent and alluring, is the source of endless war and bloodshed. Is this reality why Jesus was not looking to be yet another political king? Suffice it for our purposes that the love of your enemy is a strong demonstration of Jesus' religion-changing work (new wine), and a radical departure from the haunting story of revenge or killing the infidels (by multiple religions) throughout history.

One more matter regarding the understanding of God as the mighty, warrior king. I have witnessed how many persons and congregations emphasize praising God. It seems obvious and appropriate, and I do agree that we should praise God. Is there an issue?

A few years ago I was talking with a friend who had gone six years into the process of becoming a Catholic priest, and then lost his faith. He remains a kind, highly talented music director, and generous soul. I recall him saying, that is seems ridiculous to think of heaven as a place where all that you do is sit around and sing glory to God for eternity, as described in the book of Revelation? More than the strangeness of doing this every day in eternity is the underlying assumption that this is what God wants. Really? If God is love, is God then a giant ego, wanting to be praised forever? No, that is a residue of the old wine of God as warrior king. The God of love is different. "There is no greater love, than a person lay down their life for another," said (and did!) Jesus. We then see that such a vision of heaven and God falls short of what Jesus taught and did. Does not God want something much more than simply unending praise? God wants us to love Him/Her, to love one another, and to live a fullness of life consisting of loving relationships. That we should offer our praises to God as part of what we do is good and appropriate, but when followers seem lost in praise and heavenly escape, they can miss the call of the gospel, exemplified in Jesus' concise teaching: "So if you are offering your gift at the altar and there remember that your brother has something against you, leave your gift there before the altar. First go and be reconciled with your brother, underline>then</u> come and offer your gift." A strong proclamation that reconciliation comes before religious ritual.

Religion has been used to placate the poor and suffering, and to leave them there. To offer just pie in the sky contradicts Jesus. Yes, God will draw us to a resurrected life, but Jesus emphatically called us to serve, especially the least of these, his brothers and sisters, to be compassionate, to be merciful, to be just *in this life*. This gives the gospel flesh and blood, as Jesus had. Then people can truly know and feel God in us, through us, and beyond us. In short, I believe our understanding and our image of God is critically important, because it shapes and forms our minds and how we live out our faith in the world.

Reflection Questions

1. What is/are your images of God?

2. How does that image inform your faith and your life?

3. How do you respond to Jesus' parable of the Last Judgment (Matthew 25:31ff)?

Chapter 10. The Word of God

In the gospel of John, we hear that Jesus is the Word of God, and "in him was life." John is proclaiming Jesus and trying to connect with Greek philosophy. The Word of God is living. It is a living truth. Jesus makes the startling statement, "I am the Way and the Truth and the Life . . . and the truth shall make you free." If Jesus is the Word of God, what then is the Bible? In a phrase from one of Paul's letters, he reminds people that in the work of spreading the gospel, this new message in Jesus is being spread through people. Therefore he cautions and writes "we have this treasure (the gospel) in earthen vessels to show that the transcendent glory belongs to God." (II Corinthians 4:7ff). The earthen vessels mean human beings. All of this message, this good news, this revelation, are given to people, including the biblical writers—all of whom are limited by their humanity, their imperfection. This is vitally important and helps explain many things, including some of the horrible actions and depictions of God in the Bible, as well as the difficulties throughout church history as faithful followers debated, quarreled, even fought and killed, over the core content of the gospel and the Bible! I cannot agree with a conception that the biblical writers turned into robots or computers, simply downloading a file direct from God. When Paul writes "servants be obedient to your masters," or "women must cover their heads in church," etc., these are not eternal divine truths. These are human beings, the "earthen vessels," doing their best to guide God's people, addressing the culture of their day, limited by their humanity and the places and times in which they lived. I agree that the Bible is inspired ("Spirit-breathed"), but this treasure has come to us in earthen vessels. Therefore we can find truth and guidance in the Bible within the soil (earth) of its many books. Just as one must mine or search in the soil for gold, so also, if we search prayerfully in the Bible we can and do fine so much gold and "priceless pearls" (see Jesus' parable of the Pearl of great price). There is much of God's gold to be found. Just as Jesus set people free from a deadening religion of rules and regulations to live a life of bold, loving abandon (freedom), so also Jesus continues to enable us to see where religious tradition and practice are not in line with the God he reveals, and this includes where parts of the biblical record do not reflect God's love and purposes as revealed through Jesus. To quote author Norman Wirzba in his insightful recent book *The Way of Love*: "For Christians, Jesus is the decisive window into the love of God and the logic of scripture. In his self-offering we see where scripture has been heading and what it is ultimately about. Using another metaphor, he is the lens that brings the whole of scripture into focus."[13]

The Bible is inspired, but written by "earthen vessels"—human beings. In a similar way, God inspires throughout history, inspiring individuals to wonderful discipleship, even as they remain human. Their lives are not perfect, including so called saints. God was working in the biblical authors, but they were not rendered puppets. This is not frightening, rather it is liberating! Thus when we read in the scriptures that God authorizes genocide, we can look to Jesus, who reveals that God does not operate that way! Looking to Jesus as our "lens" is not a truth that we cannot handle.

We dare not treat the Bible casually. We are people searching diligently for the gold to be found in there! Or like people searching for "the Pearl of great price" in Jesus' parable. We have the life and work of Jesus as the measuring rod, the guide, the lens by which we do this important, interpretive work, in the Bible. Because the Bible contains the gold from God, it has authority. But finding this gold is not as simple as "the Bible says it, I believe it, and that's that." We need not be fearful that this takes away a

---

13   Wirzba, Norman. *Way of Love*. [S.l.]: HarperCollins, 2016, p. 37. http://api.overdrive.com/v1/collections/v1L1BcAAAAA2A/ products/9e90e2fe-eb7b-47a5-a5e3-8af45448a89b

foundation of biblical authority, nor do we need to create alternative foundations like the doctrine of papal infallibility—created in the 19th century. Instead, through Jesus we can decipher and more properly determine the truths in scripture, as well as in assessing religious leaders. The skills of religious scholars, lawyers, defenders of the faith, are sometimes helpful, yet they also frequently make it confusing, esoteric, and even distorted. To make this last point vivid, I turn to a short excerpt from Thomas Aquinas, considered one of the great theologians of Christianity, in which he was profoundly discussing whether two angels can occupy the same physical space simultaneously! As a person who has studied mathematics and physics, I do believe the universe is frequently more baffling, even mysterious, than we can conceive, but the angel discussion is not useful. If Aquinas wants to say that the universe, or God's realm, exceeds our understanding, okay, but he should simply state that.

Quakerism is an important and interesting branch of Christianity, and a good one to look closely at in this discussion of scripture and contemporary faith. I must mention that I taught for 33 years at a Quaker school in Philadelphia. I did not become a Quaker, but I have a deep connection and experience with this faith, and high regard for it. Through those years I attended school Quaker meeting on Thursdays, in addition to numerous other Quaker gatherings, while also attending another church on Sundays.

Many Quaker communities (called Meetings) take very seriously that the believer has a direct contact with God, by not having a minister. Worshippers sit in silence, praying, reflecting, listening and waiting to see if they perceive a word from God within. God still speaks today. God can speak in and through anyone. It happens now, as well as all through history. God is not restricted to a church, nor is God restricted to the Bible. Some biblical literalists intentionally or unintentionally believe that.

The founder of Quakerism, George Fox received revelation and inspiration from God, and went forth very boldly. Despite arrest and danger, Fox brought forth the message that Jesus is certainly God's anointed one, and that every person can directly pray to God, and receive inspiration from God—affirming that the Spirit is poured out upon all. Clergy are not required. This is not to say that they cannot be inspired leaders, but they cannot lay claim to special power, privilege, or infallibility.

The Bible teaches that the Spirit is poured out on all. Receiving God's messages, God's followers are then not called away from the world, but sent into the world to "mend the world." Or as Quaker William Penn said, "Let us see then what love can do." Quakerism is a small denomination, but it has had exceptional impact in its four centuries since Fox. It is an example of powerful new wine emerging in the 17th century. It is my observation that it is small because it is very challenging. The follower cannot simply rely on an external authority to take care of them and tell them exactly what to do, but is called to reflect regularly and deeply on the implications of a living God, who therefore still speaks to us. It is problematic to hold to the notion that God spoke two and three thousand years ago, and has gone silent. This is both a challenging and a very liberating truth. Throughout the whole process of writing this book I ask for God's help and insight, but I make no claim that I have written perfect truth—I am an earthen vessel. I have shown that my thinking is grounded in scripture, with Jesus as the defining Word of God (John 1:1ff).

It is noteworthy that Quakerism has no creeds. It does have a book of Faith and Practice, and it also has Testimonies. Testimonies include Peace, Equality, Simplicity, Community, Integrity, Stewardship, critical values and statements that inform how Quakers practice their faith. These are values not for correct doctrine, but values to act and live by, a Way of life!

My family and I attended and participated fully in other churches. It was a rich experience to have that along with my "Quaker life" as well. Early on in my teaching career I started to tell people that the William Penn Charter School (founded in 1689 by Quaker William Penn) had a soul. By that I do not mean that it was therefore holier than other secular schools, though that would make for an interesting discussion. By saying that the school had a soul is to say that it had another deep dimension to it. In the Meeting both adults and students were moved to speak, and the majority of the spoken ministry was about things of substance. The messages were often about caring, about some pain or loss in the life of the student or adult, about gratitude for others, and for being nurtured and supported by friends, teachers, and the community of the school.

Penn Charter is a compelling example of embracing new wine. When I arrived there in the Fall of 1984, the school was approaching its three hundredth anniversary, and grades three through twelve were all male—almost 100% white. By the time I retired in 2017, the school had become completely coeducational (by 1992), chosen its first African-American Head of School, Dr. Darryl Ford, in 2007, and progressed to a student body of 30% students of color, along with major new changes in how we educate in the twenty-first century.

From the soil of its Quaker philosophy, the Religious Life committee under bold leadership, transformed a good Community Service program into a robust Service-Learning program. Combining solid study of issues such as poverty, inequality and racism with hands-on service, Service-Learning (S-L) is a quantum jump beyond a simple service program. S-L was increasingly tied into the curriculum, demonstrating that the school was striving hard to live up to its philosophy of "educating students to live lives that make a difference."

Although this last example is of a school community, it can still serve as a good model of a large community evolving with the times—creating new wineskins and new wine to better serve. It is also an excellent example of a faith that believes clearly in a Living God; one who still "speaks" within, inspiring and guiding the listener.

Reflection Questions

1. Discuss the Bible having authority, though it was written by "earthen vessels."

2. Discuss Jesus as the lens through which to reveal the great truths in the scripture.

Chapter 11. Imagine!

Let us continue to imagine new wineskins for the followers of Jesus, interested in living out a simple, yet radical love ethic, and participating in Beloved Community, where the core of loving care runs deep. Jesus created a new and broad family, saying the ones who do the will of God, thus the ones who follow his teaching and example are "my mother and my brothers and my sisters." In beloved communities this fellowship of believers rises to the level of family—not secondary or distant friends. The teaching of biological family first still rises above the community of faith, but Jesus' teaching expands our family boundaries. Sharing and caring opens wider.

Disagreements and arguments will always arise, but these communities should make great efforts at understanding and reconciliation. Differences of opinion and interpretation, even wrongdoing, need not destroy the bonds of fellowship and faith, but it requires work and loving commitment. "So when you are offering your gift at the altar, if you remember that your brother or your sister has something against you, leave your gift there at the altar and go; first be reconciled to your brother or sister, and then come and offer your gift (Matthew 5: 23-24). I repeat this passage because it is epic, setting religious ritual aside and placing reconciliation first. The works of love, in community and in the world, are foremost.

While smaller beloved communities provide our foundation, there are matters that require us to think and act larger. Our actions must widen out to the world. It is necessary and wise to have aspects of our outreach and plans be discussed with other beloved communities, invoking collaboration and building connections. Thinking that our little community is the one with the best new wine, carries the danger of pride, and believing we are better or holier than others. Partnering with other communities of love makes us stronger and more effective, gives us both hope and new insight, and can help prevent us from thinking that we alone have the truth more than others. Our work is enhanced when we embrace all faithful people, and we should always be reaching out to bring in new folk. While clusters of beloved communities give us greater potential, they can also keep us humble, exposing any tendency to become narrow and exclusive, and avoiding the danger of cultism. National and regional church bodies support new ministries and build connections, but there is still a large need to address the problem of small, declining churches. Merging, or creating clusters of churches in proximity could generate excitement and hope, and new wine. An example of this occurred recently in West Philadelphia. Following a destructive fire in one small church, the Presbytery of Philadelphia thoughtfully deliberated with that church and two nearby struggling congregations, to launch one new combined congregation. Understandably, many members have a deep affection for their church and do not want to change or move, but with care and planning, they can come to see the excitement of new possibilities and the joy of fellowship with new friends. Let's come together, be bold, be creative, enjoy new faces and new places. Let the fullness of life God has given us overflow!

Churches can slide into being a friendly, charitable, country club giving a shout-out to God. It is not that that is so bad, but it comes up short on the deep call of the gospel. The surrounding culture can be a danger to the church because it can and does lead to distortions of the gospel. Sometimes it is blatant, as when the gospel becomes a message of material prosperity. More often, cultural values and norms slowly erode and distort gospel truths. For example, Christianity includes both an inner journey and outer journey. Practices of meditation, contemplation, self-realization, self-transcendence, and so on, can be beneficial, but if it doesn't lead to the outward journey into the gritty call to work for reconciliation and justice in the world, it is lacking—resonating with the majestic words of Paul in I Corinthians 13—"Even if one can speak with the tongues of angels. . . have faith so as to move mountains . . . but have not love, it is nothing." To love is to work for reconciliation, built through compassion and justice. The pursuit of the inner life must be firmly and clearly connected to the outward journey.

There is a broad appeal for inner practices for finding peace, happiness, and fulfillment—valuable goals. There is a paradox here. Jesus says that it is in serving and loving others that we find true life, declaring, "If anyone wants to become my follower, let them deny themselves and take up their cross and follow me. For those who want to save their life will lose it, and those who lose their life for my sake will find it. For what will it profit a person if he gains the whole world but forfeits his life. " (Matthew 16: 24-26). That does not mean that everyone should become a martyr—though those who have done so are impressive. The path to fullness of life is both hard and simple. In loving others, and not just our own close people, we find fullness of life—the heart of following Jesus. Recent writers have used the phrase "human flourishing" in describing the fruit of this life of love—a rich alternative phrase for fullness of life. I am happy to see increasing examples in the media of touching stories of kindness, generosity, and love. They show and demonstrate these actions bring joy and fullness of life, to both the doers and the receivers. This is also beautifully captured in the Prayer of St. Francis:

"O Master, let me not seek as much
to be consoled as to console,
to be understood as to understand,
to be loved as to love,
for it is in giving that one receives,
it is in self-forgetting that one finds,
it is in dying that one is raised to eternal life."

Ultimately, these faith or beloved communities need to move boldly outward and dive deep into the work of renewal, reconciliation, and justice. Such powerful societal witness, treading in the footsteps of Martin Luther King, Jr., gives Christianity greater weight and witness in the world, modeling the Way of Jesus in our time. People can say, "I see by your presence and your actions that you and your God truly cares for us and our struggles and our sufferings."

I recently participated in solidarity and protest in Philadelphia in the Fall of 2019, with service workers from many northeastern cities, for wages and benefits that would allow them to live above poverty. We clergy were wearing religious clothes or symbols. On several occasions I felt a tap on my arm, or a look, a few times with the comment "God is with us." Though I generally do not like to wear religious clothes, I saw in this situation, how they offered a tangible witness to God's presence and care with those who struggle with the harsh realities of poverty and injustice. Noting that the majority of those marching were people of color, it was evident that the reality and legacy of racism is still large.

This action of solidarity was organized by a remarkable faith-based organization named POWER (People Organized to Witness, Empower and Rebuild), which is an excellent example of new wine for our times. POWER launched in 2011, dedicated to faithfulness and building beloved community in Philadelphia by working to end racism and inequality and establishing justice. This movement has been spreading outward across the state of Pennsylvania. It is valuable and instructive to say more about POWER, for it can serve as an inspiration and a great example of new wineskins and wine.

POWER is an interfaith, multiracial organization, with the largest participation by Christians and Jews, consisting of roughly 50+ congregations around the city (and with a growing number beyond the city). Clergy lead and faith-based, meetings begin with prayer and faith reflections, and sometimes music. It has proven to be a very successful way for congregations, small or larger, to come together, to appreciate the fellowship and diversity of friends-in-faith, and to unite in powerful advocacy and campaigns to support and empower people—particularly the "least of these our brothers and sisters." This can be a model in many ways, including the excitement that can be found if small or shrinking churches come together for support, fellowship, worship, and being powerful disciples as described in this book. They can combine resources and start to imagine much greater possibilities of ministry.

POWER's work is organized around four campaigns addressing the needs of the people in the city and across the state. Heeding God's clear concern for the poor, outcast and marginalized, we advocate for a quality public school system, fair school funding across all 500 school districts, a living wage, affordable healthcare, environmental justice, and reform of the criminal justice system, while consistently fighting the racism that is still present in individuals and the structures and institutions of our society. All that we do is built on relationships, especially one-to-one conversations, both within our organization, and outwardly in our communities and the halls of power. We pray, sing, advocate, organize, march, and protest.

Each campaign has clergy participation and committees, that working diligently to study these issues in depth, then plan strategy and actions to move our agenda forward. As Jesus said, we strive to be "wise as serpents, but gentle as doves." We have become very visible in the city, and are well known by our political leaders, including the governor, mayor, City Council, and more and more of our state legislature. The tasks of researching, meeting, planning, taking action, following up, and moving outward are hard work. We have had significant successes, but they can take a long time, and require constant vigilance. In the process, we have come to understand those who are different from us, to find common ground, and to work side-by-side with them to do God's work in the community, creating new wine for this time.

Another long-running campaign is to obtain fair funding for all 500 school districts across Pennsylvania, for the simple reason that there is great inequality, coupled with the statistical information proving that underfunding disproportionately hurts people of color. I won't delve deeply into this campaign here, but I can utilize it in responding to the objection that such campaigns get too deeply involved in politics, possibly straying from the gospel message of Jesus. Succinctly stated, Jesus calls for the radical love of the neighbor—anyone who is suffering. He teaches that God desires that all people be treated compassionately, and wants us to flourish. Couple this with his example and his challenge of new wine and new wineskins, in every age we must ask, what does our discipleship call us to do now? A living wage and good schools are critical to living a decent life and protecting the dignity of all of God's children.

An additional fruit of this work is the bringing together of faithful people from many traditions and congregations—a diverse and wonderful community. We experience God's followers in a rich and powerful way. It's real, and it is happening.

In this time, the COVID-19 pandemic and the racial turmoil ignited by the cruel killing of George Floyd grip not only the United States, but also the world. POWER is not asleep in this moment. We are busy working even harder to ease the suffering of people, speaking boldly and opposing the inequalities and injustices which have been exacerbated by these crises, and supporting and defending the most vulnerable.

It is clear that God sends us out into the world, to love it, heal it, and to be faithful stewards. In loving the world, we obviously include the priority of loving all of God's children, including the hard work of justice. Even though in Jesus' short earthly life he did not concern himself with Caesar, his connection to the Hebrew prophets and his compassion for all people points us into the world to make it fairer and more just for all people. Deep down most people (of faith or even without faith) understand the importance of the work of leaders like King and Gandhi, and those who advocate for the benefit of the poor, neglected and marginalized. We also see that in the work of Mother Teresa, and numerous ordinary people, seeking to comfort and assist the outcasts and hurting and hungry, we have a model for following Jesus. Though the works of mercy may not change the unjust structures of society and the vast inequalities all over the world, the incredible number of these missions is massive and they bring help, hope, and love to millions. These works change hearts as well, as in the following example, a moving story of new wine.

Norman Wirzba's book *Way of Love*, offers a series of striking examples of love in action, often connected to communities, and informed by the faith of the doers. Here is one of his examples, called the story of Emma.[14] The Lord's Acre in North Carolina is a community garden launched by people of faith for the purpose of providing poison-free healthy food to poor. One year recently, some of their sweet melons started going missing, until one day they were all gone. There was a large pink bag was left behind, hanging on the shed with one melon and a bottle of beer in it. They removed the melon, but left the pink bag there. Days later, an intern from Lord's Acre saw a woman in a grocery store with the pink bag. Weeks later, the director of the Lord's Acre, Susan, saw Emma picking melons and placing them in that bag. Susan went over and engaged her in conversation. Susan began to see that Emma was becoming uncomfortable, and embarrassed, and then she became enraged, spewing out angry works at Susan for an hour. It was difficult, but Susan listened to her shame and rage. Then Emma left. Several months later, after receiving a flyer from the Lord's Acre

14   *Ibid.*, pp. 62-64

explaining that the mission of this community and garden was to feed those in need, Emma called Susan. Emma apologized. Eventually, Emma even became a volunteer at the Lord's Acre, sharing that she felt welcome and a part of the community—A poignant example of caring and reconciliation, and of a beloved faith community following Jesus' teachings and example.

Beloved communities take on different sizes, shapes, and worship styles, etc. Diversity is wonderful, in nature, in people, and in worship. We know that worship styles vary considerably. We can better appreciate those variations by worshipping with other churches and building relationships. Genuine dialogue and conversations should emerge, learning to understand and value differences. These things are happening. I am aware of several. I have participated in one called CTTT or Coming to the Table, which specifically addressed the challenges of race. I also recently read about a new initiative called Fearless Conversations of like purpose, aiming to bridge the racial divide, and address all the hurt and injustice of the past and present. As we strive for unity we become "ambassadors of reconciliation" (II Corinthians 5: 17ff), moving toward Jesus' prayer "that they all may be one." (John 17).

I know I am in the company of many when I say that music has a special place in worship and in the faith journey. Let there be not only the heritage of classical music and hymns, but also raise up all the wonderful spirituals and gospel music, as well as the ongoing creation of modern songs and hymns of faith. I continue to witness churches that want to embrace diverse people, but they do not embrace diverse music and worship, and so they often have little success. If your church lives in or near a diverse community, let your music, your worship, your discussions. and your activities diversify! It is wonderful. Into my mind flashes some amazing rose gardens, like the superb one in the Brooklyn Botanical Gardens. Roses come in many colors, each beautiful, and if you look out on a multi-colored field of roses, it is magnificent.

From the oldest days in the Bible to the future visions of heaven in Revelation, there is music on earth and in heaven. Have you been raised to great joy, and even transcendence, by music? I have, time and time again. New and varied music is, indeed, a combination of vintage wine as well as new and wonderful wine. Using all forms of music, we can move forward to overcome segregation of Sunday worship and celebrate our diversity.

Old and fading churches need to act swiftly. That their members want to stay where they are, is understandable, but not a hopeful road. Here and there, churches are combining, even across denominations. This is wonderful. Even if you do not wish to leave an old church building filled with rich memories, think of the joy, vitality, and newness of joining with others and firing up a rejuvenated faith community. You can do it! Jesus called people out from old ways and into new ones. Don't slide down and out, rise up and move forward with intentionality!

So we imagine, and happily note, that new communities, new initiatives, new wineskins have and are emerging, that people of faith (as well as many without faith) have and do unite in common causes, common charities, and common programs to serve "the least of these my brothers and sisters" (Matthew 25: 31 ff)— this is what Jesus calls us to do.

By our actions and example we can change hearts. When John the Baptist was in prison he slipped into doubt, so he sent some disciples to Jesus to ask "Are you the one who is to come," or should we look for another? Jesus answered them, "Go and tell John what you see: the blind receive their sight, the lame walk, the lepers are cleansed, the deaf hear, the dead are raised, and the poor have good news preached to them" (Matthew 11:3-5). Jesus chose not to use verbal persuasion. Rather he tells the messengers to go report the actions they were seeing, a poignant example of actions speak louder than words. And again, in the gospel of John, after trying to explain his relationship to God and sensing that some do not understand Jesus adds, or else believe me for the sake of the works themselves." (John 14: 11).

This quickly brought to mind an incident when I was 19. I got to know some of the young staff working at a family hotel on Lake George, NY. One day a group of the staff were sitting around and verbally bashing their boss behind her back—an ugly discussion. Then Dave, normally a person of few words and humble, spoke up, and everyone became silent. Dave said, "I feel sorry for Anne, she has a big and challenging job running this large resort." That's all. A stunned silence followed, and a change of atmosphere. I was so struck and moved by that incident that later that day I asked Dave about it. He responded, "I am just trying to be a Christian." That pierced into my mind and into my heart. I have not seen him since, but to this day his action and those few words deeply impacted my faith journey. As Jesus said "Go tell John what you see. . . "

Dave was one of a still growing list of people who cause me to note, here is someone who truly lives their faith—one of those whom the scriptures call the "great cloud of witnesses." When I am low, they inform and inspire me, showing that God is alive and among us now.

The God of Newness

This chapter on new wineskins feels unfinished. This is because it describes a reality that is in process; it is alive and unfolding. And it is a good thing, particularly when we note that the biblical God is one of newness. Consider the sweep of biblical history. In creation, a new world was born into this vast universe, and after several billion years, life emerged. Next we see that God formed a new people, his chosen people, and made a covenant with them. At the same time, God told His people that they were to be a light to all nations. Therefore, this God of the Hebrews is to be the God of all people.

This new people of the covenant were imperfect, and they fall into unfaithfulness, sin, and disobedience. They were conquered and enslaved by the Egyptians. Then God does a new thing and rescues them from slavery—one of the great stories of history. It is a pivotal story of liberation for all of the Abrahamic peoples: Jews, Christians, and Muslims, now constituting more than one-third of the population of the earth.

They then become a new nation—Israel. But they vacillate, sometimes good, sometimes bad, loyal and disloyal, faithful and unfaithful, moral and immoral, just and unjust. They split into two kingdoms. Ultimately, the corruptness of both nations becomes rampant. God then inspired another new effort. God raised up prophets to warn and instruct them. The prophet Isaiah declared on behalf of God:

"Behold, I am doing a new thing;

now it springs forth, do you not perceive it?"

(Isaiah 43:19)

Most of the people and kings did not turn back to God, so they both nations were conquered. Neither would rise again. The people yearned for a new king, a messiah, who would bring Israel back to glory.

Almost six centuries after the prophets, something new, small, and surprising occurred. God's next new move was found in a baby, born to a young woman named Mary. God revealed to her that this child would change the course of history, bring down the mighty and lift up the lowly, containing "good news to all people on earth," and offering salvation. God sent his Anointed One, the Messiah. In Him is the defining revelation of God's purposes. Jesus brought "new wine" to the people, and declared the need for new wineskins. He caused astonishment wherever he went, but also troubled some of the religious and political leadership. He was betrayed and executed. His followers fled in fear and grief. It appeared that this new move by God failed.

Yet in a matter of weeks, Jesus' followers re-emerged in stunning boldness and joy, declaring that Jesus was alive again. The message and movement of Jesus spread rapidly—eventually to every corner of the earth, as he had instructed.

The Bible concludes with the unusual and visionary book of Revelation. In chapter 21, John writes: "Then I saw a new heaven and a new earth; for the first heaven and first earth had passed away," and a little later he reports that God declares, "Behold, I make all things new." (Revelation 21:1,5)

Thus we see that the theme of this book to join in the call to develop new wineskins for these times is part of the ongoing narrative of God's work in this changing world. Challenging work, but the new wine of Jesus contains "the truth that sets you free."

We are witnessing the decline and fall of old wineskins, yet the new is also emerging. Will you step out and join the new work of God in this time?

Reflection Questions

1. Have you seen or been part of new initiatives? Share them.

2. Discuss individuals in your life journey, who have moved or inspired you.

Chapter 12. The Creeds and Some History

Soon after Jesus' earthly life, the church grew incredibly, despite persecutions. Many gospels were written down (many more than four), as well as various other documents, short historical books and many letters. Leaders of the young church began to meet. Working and praying and arguing (even some physical altercations), eventually choosing what the official canon of the Bible was to be. A door was closed.

The process was often tumultuous—quarrels, disagreements, rivalries, diverse interpretations of the writings and of the teachings and nature of Jesus persisted. Eventually the leaders, sometimes with pressure from Roman Emperors, held great Councils, to boil down what the new faith believes, especially around the nature and work of Jesus. Therefore, even though the biblical canon was closed, these Councils set out to interpret, explain and define the core meaning of Christianity. During the course of these events, the Emperor Constantine approved and allowed Christianity into the Empire in 325 CE, and in 386 CE the Emperor Theodosius established Christianity as the religion of the Roman Empire. The consequences of the adoption of Christianity by the empire were vast. The church took on some of the forms of empire, and became itself a large, wealthy, and powerful institution.

Two short statements were soon declared the beliefs of the Church, the Nicene and the Apostle's Creed, and both with a major omission by no mention of the earthly teaching and ministry of Jesus. This led to a shift towards Christianity becoming an assent to theological / philosophical assertions, that Jesus did not propose. Jesus' Way of life moves to a back seat.

Fortunately, throughout history impressive voices have spoken up to bring the earthly Jesus back into the center of

Christianity. This renewed wine restored the new wine that Jesus brought, establishing the meaning of Jesus for a new epoch of history. The 16th century reformers are the most well known—Luther, Calvin, Knox—but there were others before them, and there have been more since then. In modern times we have voices from those oppressed—women, people of color, including some from Africa and South America, who have spoken up to challenge both political leaders and religious leaders who ignore or try to keep them quiet, offering them only pie in the sky.

God cannot be bound by Canon Law, or creeds, or even blind adherence to the Bible. Those writings can be useful, but weeds of religious paraphernalia keep growing back and choking the life-giving vitality of Jesus' teaching and Way. Unfortunately, control and power drive many religious leaders to squelch new voices, blurring the truth that sets you free.

Of course, some new voices have been false, distorted, even deranged, so the church must prayerfully discern the faithfulness of a new voice or movement. In recent centuries, examples on the positive side include, George Fox and the Quakers—who believe God continues to speak within us with new revelation—and John Woolman in the 1700s who traveled around the country and speaking out against slavery. There is Sojourner Truth and John Wesley and others who led revival, reform, and an elevated mission of social concern. In the 19th century, The Social Gospel of Walter Rauschenbush and others, pushed outward into fuller involvement within society. Quite a few women, especially in Quakerism in the 19th and 20th centuries, such as Lucretia Mott, Elizabeth Cady Stanton, and Susan B. Anthony brought the new wine of women's rights and equality! In our time, newer prophets and voices include Martin Luther King, Gandhi, Archbishop Oscar Romero, Bishop Tutu, Gustavo Guitierrez, as well as countless authors of the last two centuries have cried out from countries all over the world, often in behalf of God's suffering children, calling us to adjust, correct or broaden our understanding of who and what Jesus is and means, and to remind us of the work that he calls us to do today.

The voices above, and many others (including myself) did not attempt to add a text to the Bible, but through their insights we re-discover the wonderful, liberating messages in the text—which are the grounds for a strong critique of status quo Christianity, which is once again an example of culturally warped Christianity. In his time, Kierkegaard called the status quo church "Christendom," in order to differentiate it from the truly engaged Way of Jesus. The sources and inspiration for this ongoing process of weeding and cleansing are the prophets and Jesus in their time. Yet the weeds and the brambles keep coming back. In our faith, which holds Jesus to be authoritative, he has to be the lens for us to study scripture and to understand God. We thank God for this.

Will we strive to go forward with Jesus? Yet there is a conundrum to consider: Many Christian folk constantly like to say his name and to lose themselves in saying "praise Jesus." To praise him is a good and wonderful thing, yet he warns us: "Not everyone who says to me "Lord, Lord" will enter the kingdom of heaven, but only the one who does the will of my Father in heaven. On that day many will say to me, 'Lord, Lord, did we not prophesy in your name, and cast our demons in your name, and do many deeds of power in your name?' Then I will declare to them, I never knew you, go away from me, you evildoers" (Matt 7: 21-23).

Isn't that clear? Jesus rejects a recitation of creeds, a verbal discipleship without the actions of love. It is not enough to say his name a lot.

Similarly, Jesus is not interested in thousands of pages of theology that debates and tries to define him. He would not endorse this debate, would likely be angry about it! Jesus' theologizing was given through short, startling parables, and direct, piercing ethical teachings on how to treat one another, embedded in a walking ministry of forgiving, healing, and loving. Then he would say, "Follow me."—utter simplicity. And for a daily prayer he gave us the Abba Prayer (Lord's Prayer), along with the command to get out there and love God and your neighbor.

Neither scripture nor Jesus say that at the end of times he will ask, "Here is the million dollar question, can you explain the nature of my Being? Be careful, your answer will be the difference between heaven and torture in a fiery hell." No! The parable in Matthew 25 tells us what God and Jesus are truly interested in and what they will ask on the day of Judgment. Jesus said he wants to know if you cared for all God's children, and especially the poor and sick and hungry and imprisoned. Read the whole parable for its full strength. This parable is one that I have mentioned again, because of a great need to address the problem I call "Jesus without Jesus." He instructs us to follow him and "do all that I have commanded," and as hard as that can be, in this path of forgiveness and love we will find joy and fullness of life—beginning now.

The works of mercy and justice give earthly support to the central work of reconciliation offered by God. Paul writes in 2 Corinthians 5:19. "God was in Christ, reconciling the world to Himself." I propose that we focus on "God was in Christ" not as a philosophical-theological assertion, but rather as a declaration that God was working in and through Jesus in his message and actions, towards the goal of reconciliation and redemption. While this can lead back to the ancient debates, don't; turn instead to Jesus the Christ, Jesus as God's Anointed. Live by and in his message of forgiveness and freedom and love, unencumbered by a mass of laws and theologies. To successfully do this requires the support of a beloved community.

All the gospels declare that the Messiah of God has come in Jesus. His life and works amazed the crowds. More than that, they proclaim that after he was crucified, he rose again to glory.

Paul has more good news. In addressing the tension and difficulties and divisions that arose among the Jews and Gentiles he proclaims: "For he (Christ) is our peace; in his flesh he has made both groups into one and has broken down the dividing wall between us. He has abolished the law with its commandments and ordinances; that he might create in himself one new humanity in place of the two, thus making peace, and might reconcile both groups to God in one body through the Cross, thus putting to death that hostility through it." (Ephesians 2: 14-16).

Jesus, the Christ, is the Reconciler, reaching out with a world embrace. If we do not let Jesus be restricted to old creedal debates, we can affirm what is happening now in many places. Many Christians are involved in interfaith work not always trying to convert everyone, but working together for God and affirming that the God of love, the God of Jesus, has spoken in Judaism, in Christianity, as well as in other places and other religions. This is an extension of the reconciling work of God to God's children in different places and faiths. God does not care more about creeds than about his other children throughout the world. Jesus will not be contained, or used again to support holy wars. That is not the Way of Jesus. This is more Good News. We do not diminish Jesus by saying that he has come for all people, and that the God of whom he spoke and prayed to, is God of all. In the gospel of John, Jesus says, "And I, if I be lifted up, will draw all people to myself" (John 12:32). Does this not lend itself more readily to interfaith cooperation?—without requiring that all the Others first become one of us— which is a trap for nearly all the major religions.

The story of the Samaritan woman at the well in John chapter 4 is relevant and ripe on the call to reach out beyond the bounds of one's own group. From the start, Jesus is defying the rules of his culture and tradition by interacting again with a woman. Not only that, she is from a despised group—the Samaritans. He asks her for water. She is surprised that he speaks to her, but daringly engages him, stating that both Jews and Samaritans are waiting for the Messiah, to which Jesus replies "I am he." In this exchange, he declares that "God is spirit" and is not limited to Jerusalem, or any one place, and the that time is coming when any who want to worship God can do so "in spirit and in truth."

To protect Jesus and his message from drowning in theologies and religious—Jesus without Jesus—we have to keep our eyes on the one who walked the earth, who revealed so much to us, and who conquered death! He calls us to respond to his commandments and message of bold love, and not to fixate on philosophical or theological quandaries. Jesus and God care about all people, about compassion, healing, returning home to a loving God, of working for a new Community of God—which is unlike the kingdoms of this world.

It was not Jesus who kept raising hypothetical and theological questions—it was the religious leaders following him around. He usually answered with a story or parable, or succinct ethical teachings, which within the context of the event and the times, evoked a jolt, a surprise—an unexpected turn. They served to jolt people out of their blindness or prejudice, and showed us how God wants us to live, instead of supplying answers for a theological final exam at the end of life. The final exam is, were you loving, compassionate, forgiving, and just—which is central to the meaning of following Jesus?

Now that could be an intimidating final exam! However, the magnificent Good News is that he tells us that God is loving and forgiving. God forgives us. Love and forgiveness are free, which is what is meant by grace. Yet we must not treat grace as cheap. Rather, in gratitude, joy and freedom, love boldly and deeply. If we let this gospel, this good news, into our hearts and minds, sincerely asking for forgiveness when we fall, we can be confident of God's forgiving love for us. Confident. That is the truth that sets us free, that is the dynamic that liberates us to live without being haunted and beaten down by our weaknesses, faults, and bad deeds. Just get out there and live with loving abandon. If you fall, ask for forgiveness and "keep on keepin' on," joined with all of God's children of like purpose spreading and building the Beloved Community of God. Remember the parables calling us to be "doers of his word."

Reflection Questions

1. Discuss Matthew 25, on what Jesus will look for in the Day of Judgment.

2. Is this emphasis on Jesus' Way different from what you were, or were not taught? Discuss.

Chapter 13. A Haunting Question

The powerful chapter of the Grand Inquisitor in Dosto-yevsky's *Brothers Karamazov* raises for me a haunting question: whether we should be challenging old assumptions and beliefs, or leaving people alone in the shaky comfort of their ancient world-view and faith, whatever it may be.

In this chapter, Dostoyevsky creates an imagined scene of Jesus returning during the time of the Inquisition. Jesus is captured and jailed by the Grand Inquisitor, who is a Cardinal in the church.

The Grand Inquisitor posits that people cannot handle the freedom Christ tries to give them, a profound version of the mem-orable movie question "you can't handle the truth" in the movie "A Few Good Men." This haunting question could also be called "the pastoral question," or consideration. Let me explain. Most people find security in their beliefs, but should we remain silent when such beliefs push credulity, and which harm the case for religious faith. Two that raise concern are, "everything happens for a reason" or "it is all a part of God's plan," which allows the believer to conclude that there is no need to worry about what is going on in the world. They can gloss over, avoid, or evade the major and many horrors of history, including the fact that the 20th century was the deadliest century of all time . They can blithely say, or unconsciously imply, that the large scale slaughter of people killed in war and genocide, is all part of the plan—God's plan. What kind of plan is that? This ugly reality also makes it impossible to say everything is getting better and better. Some people place this all in the container of, "it is all human evil," therefore, sad as it might be, the majority of humankind is destined for eternal hell and torment. That brutal conclusion combined with an unrelenting and violent history sounds like a deluge of bad news that drives people away from religion, or to live in fear, or in a seem-ingly happy bubble thinking "at least I am saved."

Still others of the faithful seem to leapfrog over or simply disregard the dark and harsh aspects of their religious tradition—don't discuss it, don't think about it. One rests with, "I can be forgiven and I will be all right. That is enough, I am set." And finally, there is a large group of Christians who live by, "I simply follow the instructions of the church, and get on with my life." They keep busy with daily life, do a few good deeds, and rarely concern themselves with a Christianity that calls for a deeper discipleship of engaged love and justice.

This book asserts that avoiding the deeper call of reconciliation and justice is not what we hear from Jesus and the prophets. The pastoral question above responds: Leave religious leaders free to offer comforting versions of Christianity, even though they ignore much of the teachings and call of Jesus. Let people get on with their lives, leave them to believe as they wish and be comforted—or as some say, believe whatever floats your boat. After all, most people encounter their share of personal struggles, hardships, heartaches, so they can't handle the tougher road of discipleship. Consequently, the Grand Inquisitor locks Jesus up, out of his belief that he knows people better than Jesus, in order to prevent Jesus from firing up his movement again with the "truth that will set you free,"- because they cannot handle it.

As I consider this pastoral question of leaving people with whatever interpretation of Christianity makes them feel secure or good, I reflect back on the following: Even though being faithful to the Jesus we see in the gospels is about following a Way of Life, not about passing a test on creeds and orthodoxy, I cannot maintain that God (of Love) will reject people for incorrect beliefs. In effect, if you fail the doctrines and creeds test, you are going to burn forever. Heavens No.

Does that mean anything goes? That seems like a legitimate challenge. Jesus offers a powerful paradox: Jesus is abundantly forgiving of those who genuinely seek it (forgive even "seventy times seven times" he says), yet he is quite demanding. He does not call for a recitation of belief, but rather for a portfolio of love. . . after all "everyone who loves knows God, for God is love" (I John 4:7ff). We have to believe deeply and truly that God is love, the very One who calls us to love God and our neighbors. To believe deeply in love is to do love, and we know that can be hard. It runs deeper than much of what we hear proclaimed.

This leaves us with a thorny issue. If we do not also choose to skip over difficult parts of scripture, even in the New Testament, then how can we protest against those who skip over the numerous problems in the older Testament? For example, in Jesus' parable of the The Last Judgment found in Matthew 25, Jesus declares to those on his left hand, "You that are accursed, depart from me into the eternal fire prepared for the devil and his angels; for I was hungry and you gave me no food, I was thirsty and you have me nothing to drink, I was a stranger and you did not welcome me, naked and you did not give me clothing, sick and in prison and you did not come to visit me. . . for as you did not do it to one of the least of these, you did not do it unto me." This could fit with Jesus' Way of Love, in that it condemns those who are not loving. But it poses a quandary: Would the God of love take some of his children who have been un-loving and cast them into eternal torment. Endless agony for finite evil? Some punishment could be appropriate, but eternal torture? Does that force me into a position which does not fit with my overall understanding of Christianity? For it then appears that Christianity is not a "joyful love story," for if you miss the measure of love or fail the creed test, you will be cast out, beaten, and burned forever.

Is there a way out or a way through? My answer may be a modern adaptation of Blaise Pascal's famous "Great Wager." Brief-ly, in that discussion Pascal debates on faith versus no faith, making the case that it is more sensible to choose faith, for what can you lose with that choice? If there is nothing else, you disappear into a meaningless universe. If there is God, then you made the right choice. Quite logical, but there is a better answer, a more Jesus-like proposal. My great wager, or decision of faith, is that, looking at the whole of the New Testament, I make the wager that God is love to be the highest truth, prompted by statements of Jesus and also of Paul. Paul declared, "three things endure, faith, hope and love, and the greatest of these is love." And, "if I understand all mysteries and all knowledge, and if I have all faith so as to remove mountains, but do not have love, I am nothing" (I Corinthians 13). Coupled with Jesus telling us that the two Great Commandments are love God and love your neighbor as yourself. This God of love will not torch the majority of the human race—His creation.

The person of Jesus also leads to mystery—which cannot be answered by philosophy or science. The gospels show us the compelling life of Jesus. If he was truly human, then Jesus did not know everything (which he actually asserted on a couple of occasions). So I do not think he new quantum physics and the theory of relativity, or as I recently heard stated "could Jesus speak Mandarin?" I think that playfully makes the point. He accepted the worldview of his time, with heaven above, hell below, and earth in between. His invocation of hell expressed real outrage at the mistreatment of any of God's children, and at lack of compassion. People do need to be screamed at sometimes. In a time of Judgment, as in a time of trial and punishment, people could be called to account, by reviewing the evil or heartlessness they once did. That would be painful, a hard punishment, but it can also be redemptive. People would have to reckon with their lovelessness, to feel and witness it for a while—but not infinitely, nor sadistically. Finite and hard, until they come to utter, "I see and feel the pain I have caused, forgive me I pray," and at God's moment, brought back to a place of timeless love. I place my Wager on this God of love.

In the Christian tradition we believe that Jesus is The Christ. This means he is God's anointed one, or Messiah. That is an affirmation of the God of love. We can count on it. We can rejoice. What good and liberating news!

Reflection Questions

1. Do you think that everyday people can handle the truth that sets you free? Explain.

2. What do you make of the paradox that the good news of Jesus is simple—set free by forgiveness and called to a Way and a life of love—yet hard at the same time?

Chapter 14. An Important Obstacle

I want to discuss a problem that often, perhaps unintentionally, contributes to despair, inaction, hopelessness, and leads to maintaining the status quo of ongoing divisions, hate, racism, and twisted or inaccurate perceptions of people and reality. It can lead to discouragement and people throwing up their hands and deciding it is useless to try and change the world. It is what I call the trap or quicksand of the news and media. This seeming tangent impacts what we think and how we live and act. It also impacts our faith, or lack of it.

Since at least the late 1800s yellow journalism combined with a widespread fascination with what is sensational, extraordinary, heart-wrenching, bloody and startling, has led news reporting to want to bring these events into the news. It makes eye-catching headlines, gets attention and sells. Add to that, now with all our modern technologies, we are able to learn of innumerable events around the world extremely rapidly. Here is the result, in a world now approaching 8 billion people, even if the probability (and I am talking in real mathematical terms—I was a math major in college) of a murder, or a clash between neighboring countries is extremely small, that tiny percentage of 8 billion is still a large number. You may be amazed by what follows. I saw a statistic that said the worldwide murder rate was 6.2 per 100,000 people in 2012—that is less than one-hundreth of one percent. One-hundreth of one percent! Miniscule. However, when we multiply that times 7.7 billion people we get 477,000 murders per year, a very large number! That means, mathematically speaking and in reality, that every day we can *always* find many murders occurring, as well as conflicts, catastrophes, accidents, floods, fires, and so on, around the globe and in our country. Since the news wants to bring the sensational, tragic, graphic and heart rending, we get this horror show every single day—no exceptions ever! This vividly and easily creates a picture of a world gone to hell, a world of violence and near chaos.

Friends, it is a world of way too much violence, but the media by virtue of what it believes it must tell us, creates a profoundly distorted sense of reality. It is not fake news! But it is a great distortion of every day reality. That is a troubling truth. We probably do not realize how much our subconscious and conscious minds have absorbed and accepted a violent, explosive, turbulent reality. I don't think we can overstate this. I frequently fight with it personally. I am not always obsessed with the news as it seems so many are these days, nevertheless I do watch the news because I do want to know what is going on. I imagine that quite a few people have lost their faith over this troubling, but selective, and very incomplete reality. Now since these events are real, one might then ask, why can you call it distorted? The answer is mathematical, real numbers. The vast, vast majority of people live rather ordinary, quiet daily lives, with both their joys and sorrows. But we only get a small glimpse of that. We are drawn to the explosive news, to the very small percentage, to a very small part of the total picture of life on our planet. It is that simple, the news focuses on a very small slice of reality. However, this visual, emotional, harsh and crazy reality is so powerful and memorable when shown to us on TV and in pictures, that it has a major effect on not only our intellect, but much more profoundly on our emotional system. That is what often drives our lives. Add to that the power of our cell phones, we can literally drown ourselves in this darkness 24/7 if we want to, or have become addicted to. It is not hard to see why many people can say, "you say there is a loving God, but just look at the world!" That is a fair challenge, but it is frequently driven by the powerful, distorted presentation of life in the media.

A similar observation can be made about the big picture of history. Though from many years ago, I still remember the following passage from two historians, a husband and wife team named Will and Ariel Durant, who were rather well known back then. They wrote eleven massive volumes entitled *The Story of Civilization*, covering ancient civilizations and moving all the way through to the 19ᵗʰ century. After this incredible accomplishment, they then wrote a short book called *The Lessons of History*. Obviously they had taken a long, well researched look at history. The following quote impressed me deeply:

> We must remind ourselves again that history as usually written (*peccavimus*) is quite different from history as usually lived: the historian records the exceptional. If all those individuals who had no Boswell had found their numerically proportionate place in the pages of historians we should have a duller but juster view of the past and of man. Behind the red façade of war and politics, misfortune and poverty, adultery and divorce, murder and suicide, were millions of orderly homes, men and women kindly and affectionate, troubled and happy with children. Even in recorded history we find so many instances of goodness, even of nobility, that we can forgive, though not forget, the sins. The gifts of charity have almost equaled the cruelties of battlefields and jails. [15]

Since that was written, the exponential growth of technologies such as the cellphone can slide us into a dark mindset and perception of the world more than the Durants could have imagined! There is no denying the bad events, but it highlights such a small slice of reality—it is like showing photographs of damaged trees and missing the view of the whole beautiful forest.

15   Durant, Ariel, and Will Durant. *The Lessons of History*. New York: Simon & Schuster, 2014.

I am in the midst of the final editing of this book in the middle of the coronavirus pandemic of 2020. It is a troubling challenge, and we are not yet out of it. Major epidemics have happened before, but they were before the age of jet flight that has radically shrunk the world and brought us into closer contact. Consequently, this epidemic quickly became a pandemic. Even with a faith perspective, we cannot dismiss this simply as one of those random, bad events. I am also glad that I have not been hearing erratic voices declaring that this is God's wrath or punishment. This book emerged before this pandemic and it is built on the revelation of God through Jesus which powerfully declares that God is love—God earnestly seeks to forgive and welcome back all of his people. That God is not a wrathful, volatile, jealous king, smiting people as they go wrong.

The mathematical insight of which I have spoken can still help with correcting the distortion that history is mostly a horror show. It does for me. It helps. I certainly am still deeply troubled by what I see in the world, so I am far from walking around in a mathematically induced happy bubble. Indeed, if one cares about people and the world, then one will be troubled. However, try to keep the big truth in mind, the millions of happy homes that the Durants speak of, and the ocean of kindnesses and good deeds occurring every day! In this very pandemic, the deeds of sacrifice (healthcare and other frontline workers), compassion, sharing and kindness have been an epidemic of love. It is magnificent, and my deep prayer is that we would be this loving, generous, and bold even after the pandemic fades out.

I have taken a variety of measures to help keep me going forward in a troubled world. One of the things I have done is write myself small meditations that remind me of the larger realities of love and faith, rarely reported in the media.

Here is one image or analogy I wrote forty years ago, and still find it truthful and helpful. I call it God's Gulf Stream of Love.

It is this: The Gulf Stream is a large current of warm water that flows from the south where the Gulf of Mexico and the Atlantic ocean meet. It travels north relatively close to the United States, and then slants across the Atlantic towards England and Ireland, and perhaps beyond. Within that warm current there is abundant marine life, and the Gulf Stream keeps many northern areas considerably warmer than it would be without the warm air rising from the warm waters. On the surface, the ocean remains rough and turbulent, hiding the abundant life found beneath. For me this is a helpful image of God's work of love almost hidden beneath the turbulence of trouble and violence in the world and magnified by the media. This image might be critiqued, but it is not offered as a sort of scientific answer to the problem of world violence and hardship. Rather it contains for me a memorable image that offers a larger perspective, an additional dimension, to what we see on the surface of life. It also is similar to the above quote from the historians Will and Ariel Durant.

Turning to Jesus and the Prophets, we have a message of very good news, which should send us out on the challenging road of discipleship, singing, praying, doing acts of kindness and stepping up to the call of justice and reconciliation. We must also keep our eyes open to the wonderful initiatives and ministries already underway, and find or create new initiatives of love, reconciliation and justice . As the wonderful spiritual says, "Keep your eyes on the prize. . . Hold on" and continue to pray and work for more new wineskins.

Reflection Questions

1. Discuss the idea that media news, by common practice, gives us a distorted (not false), but very incomplete view of reality?

Chapter 15. The Ultimate Question

This book is centered in following Jesus by living according to what Jesus taught and demonstrated, profoundly concerned with loving our neighbors and being compassionate and just. This closing chapter is not new wine. But it is the linchpin or foundation of Christianity. Paul, the author of much of the New Testament, made the bold proclamation, "If Christ be not raised, then our faith is in vain" (I Corinthians 15:12-17) . The ultimate question then is, what about the Resurrection?

We cannot prove that the Resurrection is true. Additionally, many educated people believe that resurrection is not scientifically possible. So, I would like to offer an analogy from science that I find very compelling for my belief in the Resurrection of Jesus. I preface this analogy with a brief biographical note. My undergraduate degree was a major in mathematics and a minor in Physics. I enjoy physics, with a particular passion for the area of physics called cosmology. My study of modern physics has led me to see a universe so vast, strange, wonderful, paradoxical, awe-inspiring, that I was and am persuaded that something more is needed to make sense of it. I echo the great awe described by the Psalmist in Psalm 8.

In the 19th century physicists started to look at an ancient Greek idea that the world was made of very small particles called atoms. They pursued this hypothesis even though no one had ever seen an atom, because they are so small that no one had the capability to see them. They posited the existence of atoms because their existence explained much about how the universe behaves. Since then the results and evidence of atomic theory are massive, thereby confirming the unseen reality of atoms, and many other nuclear particles. Similarly, we do not see people rising from the dead. However, what everyone has observed is that after this wandering preacher named Jesus had a short ministry and was then crucified and buried, astounding events and results followed. A significant number of people claimed to have seen him, declaring that "He is alive." Following that there was an incredible explosion—his frightened and scattered followers suddenly became emboldened, claiming to have seen Jesus, and going forth despite severe persecutions by the Roman Empire and rejection by others. They proclaimed this message, and it spread like a wild fire—like an atomic love bomb. Their practices of love and caring earned them the reputation as people of the Way. This historical phenomenon indicates that something dramatic, powerful and life-changing occurred following the crucifixion—a different type of "Big Bang." It has spread to every corner of the globe. Despite inevitable human failings, millions, now billions, have given their lives over to God through Jesus, some to the point of great sacrifice and even death. Who would die for a hoax? Something extraordinary happened, Christianity came into being, and it changed the course of history.

Without resurrection then this life, including living by Jesus' Way, is at best a noble tragedy. Paul proclaims the Resurrection, exclaiming, "Death is swallowed up in victory. Thanks be to God who gives us the victory in Christ Jesus." In contrast to death extinguishing all life– everyone we love or who loves us, the good and the bad, all dissolves, some as early as in miscarriages, others in a life of much suffering, multitudes in poverty, and some percentage who, perhaps, have a life of considerable happiness and material fortune. . . but they too die, and all accomplishments fade away into nothingness. This led the writer of Ecclesiastes to repeatedly declare "all is vanity, a striving after wind."

There is still more that my study of science does to bolster my faith and lead me to the conclusion that there is More than meets the eye, or telescope or microscope—and that this More is something wonderful. First, in Einstein's Theory of Relativity the equation for time shows that *time slows down as you approach the speed of light—called time dilation.* During space flight, scientists were able to verify time dilation—less time transpired on the rocket than on earth! Additionally, the equation indicates that if you reach the speed of light, time would come to a stand. Well, if time stops, do you then rest in an eternal moment—eternity? No doubt some will object, but my response to that objection is, I am not saying that this is a proof of eternity, only that this is one of various aspects of modern physics that are quite astonishing and mind-boggling—there is a relativity of time! It makes me think of the Psalmist again, who says of God, "A thousand years are as one night to Thee O God." (Psalm 90:4), a poetic rendering of the relativity of time.

God said, "Let there be light." Light deserves great attention. Traveling at 186,000 miles per <u>second</u>, which is seven and a half times around the earth in one second, light travels nearly 5 trillion miles in a single year. Astronomers tell us that stars and galaxies are *hundreds of millions* of *light years* away! We can say that, but we really can't conceive it—go ahead if you wish, and compute how many miles there are in one hundred million light years. Truly mind-boggling, the universe is inconceivably large.

Light consists of particles called photons, but these particles have no mass? How can you have a particle with no mass? Light is special and crucial, without it there would be no life as we know it.

I have been aware of these things for a long time, but only recently did the following thought come to mind: It appears as if light is eternal, for this simple reason. Referring to various stars, scientists state that many of the stars we observe in our telescopes are probably long gone—burned out. The light we observe originated perhaps hundreds of millions of years ago. The star may have collapsed into what is called a black hole. The light has been traveling for many millions of years and trillions of miles—it seems virtually eternal. Only the light that collides with something stops, such as the earth. On earth it is absorbed, and offers tremendous energy, and it makes life possible. Light is probably our greatest hope for clean energy.

Does light stop at the edge of the universe? How can there be an edge to the universe? What would be/is on the other side of the edge? Not to mention that they have found that the universe is expanding at super speeds and also accelerating? Sounds crazy.

One more observation about light: Perhaps the most famous equation in physics is $E = mc^2$, and arguably the most foundational equation of all. E is Energy, m is mass (matter), and c is the speed of light. What it fundamentally says is that from a piece of matter you can get an enormous amount of energy! Remember the speed of light is a very big number (186,000 mps) and when you square it, it makes a huge number. A small amount of matter translates into an enormous amount of energy. If one wonders, how do we know that is true? The answer is, look at atomic energy and the atomic bomb—what they can do with only a small amount of matter. That is an atomic answer!

Light is central to the universe, and a major metaphor in faith. This is not a proof, but I find that the universe brings awe and wonder, and begs for explanation.

An agnostic Phd scientist friend of mine says he has no answer as to how or where the original hydrogen for the Big Bang came from. I affirm the Big Bang Theory, but important questions remain. How did that hydrogen come into existence? Why is there something rather than nothing? Or why is there anything? Our minds yearn for explanation and sense. Does senselessness make sense? Meditate on that—or maybe that is a sinkhole to avoid. I find that all this only becomes intelligible if there is something More, and something greater, behind it all. This is a modern variation on an old case for the existence of God—that's okay.

Additionally, I don't care how much our knowledge grows about life and the world, when you see this beautiful and incredibly complex being emerge from the womb after 9 months, it is again and again, awe-inspiring, and almost beyond belief.

I could say more, but will wrap it up here. Science practically shouts to us that the universe is unbelievable. In the end, I find that this universe is more explainable and understandable with a Higher Intelligence than without one. And then, Jesus tells us that this Higher Intelligence is God—not just any God, but the God of Love, and the God who called the ancient Hebrews to be a witness and a light unto the nations!

Thus I do believe in the Resurrection. I also believe that it is unwise to speculate too much about the nature of resurrection. Leave it as St. Paul says "there are terrestrial bodies and there are celestial bodies," a beautiful way to say that it is a mystery, as he also says. Let it be! It is enough for me so I can say with the faithful, "He lives!" and because of that we too shall live after death! And perhaps we can come to the realization of Julian of Norwich who said, "And all shall be well. And all shall be well. And all manner of thing shall be well."

Reflection Questions

1. Whether or not you may be a mathematics and physics fan, do the wonders of this universe tie into your faith? Discuss.

2. Discuss the reality that this wandering Jewish preacher lived a short life, and had a very short ministry, cut off by execution by the Roman Empire, but changed the course of history—reaching every corner of the earth with over 2 billion adherents at this time.

Joyful Epilogue

I wanted my book to have a certain intensity and urgency, reflecting the full dimensions of Jesus' call to discipleship amidst the distortions or very deficient displays of Christianity in the world. And I have kept the book short because I am convinced that being a follower of Jesus does not require a theology degree, nor does it need long and dense systematic theologies. The gospel is simple, while profound. With both a salute and a protest, to the profound theologians of the past who have written numerous volumes, I remind us that Jesus primarily taught with parables and terse ethical commands, healing along the way, and calls of "Follow me." He said that His Way of discipleship would be tough, because it is tough to love not only friends but also enemies, to love sinners as well as saints, to love the broken and outcast as well as the successful and prominent, to love those who are despairing as well as those who are hopeful. And while Jesus declared that His Way is hard, but simultaneously that God is ultimately Grace-Full—profoundly forgiving, doggedly determined to find and rescue sinners and heal the broken, lift up the poor, and love and save us all, as a Gift—despite our failings.

Jesus called us to love, to do the compassionate thing, the generous thing, the right thing, the just thing. It is not about earning or scratching our way to God. It should and can be a response of gratitude for the gifts and promises of God. We can stretch to do the works of love out of the great Joy that God offers us the gift of healing, fullness of life, and salvation, setting us free to live in the newness of life in Christ. Faith is not centered in ceremony—those are dressings that can be used, as long as they don't become the main course. The gospel dwells in the wonderful paradox of simplicity with profundity. Because the gospel is a "love thing" it needs to dwell in community, beloved community, that will cause people to observe, see how they care for one another, and then move out into the world to make it better.

How can one do this believing in a God, said to be loving, yet portrayed frequently as angry, jealous, and punitive? Surely God is angry with human evil, but the final and triumphant word is God's redeeming love. The media focus on what is sensational, catastrophic, and wrong makes that difficult to see. The actions of love exceed those of evil. If we want to see God, we must tune in and look for love, finding that God emerges everywhere. No matter how bad the event, there immediately arise loving people and loving actions, pointing us to the realization that that is where God can be found in the mix.

In the climax of *Les Miserables*, Jean Valjean utters the words, "to love another is to see the face of God." Do we not know this, and know it deeper than just our intellect? When we observe love overcoming suffering, evil, hate, injustice, we are moved at our core, our heart, the place of the indwellingness of God. "Three things endure, faith, hope, and love. But the greatest of these is love" (I Corinthians 13).

Acknowledgments

It has been a joy to have friends who unhesitatingly agreed to read my manuscript and offer feedback. They took on and completed the task with graciousness, candor, and encouragement. There is no question that they helped improve the book. They lifted my spirit time and again, and helped keep me moving forward. I greatly appreciate their work and support, and am happy with the results.

My deep gratitude to Jim Ballengee, Nancy Elmore, Irene McHenry, Jeff Singleton, Michael Moulton, Karin Crawford, Howard Friend, Brian Gibson, Bill Kashatus, Julia Sheetz, and to my talented, encouraging, and gracious taskmaster—my editor David Colin Carr. When I finished my first draft I did not realize how much more work was ahead, but David and these friends were superb teammates. Thank you.

Made in the USA
Middletown, DE
24 July 2020